Creative at Work

501 ideas for creating a happy, productive workplace

Henry Stewart

Foreword by Stuart Crainer, Co-founder, Thinkers50

First published in the United Kingdom by Happy

Richard Dolan House, 9 Alie Street, London E1 8DE

Copyright © Henry Stewart 2023

All rights reserved

Feel free to borrow, copy or nick any of the ideas in this book.

ISBN: 9798399751351

"A fabulous array of entirely doable ideas that could transform your company and your teams' lives."
Adrienne Rogers, NHS England

"Chock full of proven ideas to create happier, more productive workplaces. Henry has done the hard work of gathering ideas from transformational organisations far and wide."
Chris MacQueen, Stroke Association

"You come away feeling like you went on sixteen management courses with some of the most well-established, forward-thinking consultancy companies in the world. When you have dedicated your professional life to the charity sector – that's a gift!"
Jude Williams, Literacy Pirates

"An invaluable handbook for a modern, empowered workplace – buzzing after only a few chapters. So many to 'nick' and adapt – some with caution – you might release a surge of energy!"
Margaret Burnside, Cake PD

"Whether you read from end to end, or dip for inspiration, you will always find a nugget you can use and use straight away."
Laura Dawson, LSE

"A treasure trove, not just of inspiring quotes, but particularly practical examples of what companies and organisations of all kinds and in all sectors, actually do – as can you."
Koenraad Van Brabant, Global Mentoring Initiative

Contents

Foreword 7

Introduction 9

The Happy Manifesto: 10 Principles for a Great Workplace 11

Case Study: Happy **13**

1. Trust Your People 16

Trust-based workplaces 16
Pre-approval 20
Involve your people 25
As a manager, make few or no decisions 29
The Advice Process 32
Trade unions are your friends 34
Setting salaries in a trust-based workplace 35

Case Study: Buurtzorg **37**

2. Make Your People Feel Good 40

Build relationships 40
Joy at work 44
Happiness as a focus 46
Fulfilling dreams 48
Replace appraisals 53
Recognition 57
Staff first, customers second 59
Challenge 60

Case Study: Semco **61**

3. Freedom within Guidelines 64

Get people to set their own targets 66
Systems not rules 69
Innovation 70
Feedback 71

Case Study: Reddico **73**

4. Be Open and Transparent **77**

Communication 81
Open salaries 84

Case Study: Belgian Federal Office of Social Affairs **85**

5. Recruit for Attitude, Train for Skill **87**

Recruit for attitude 87
Get people to do the job in the interview 90
Collaborative hiring 92
Induction 99
Promotion 100
Moving people on 101

Case Study: Toyota **103**

6. Celebrate Mistakes **108**

Case Study: Google **113**

7. Community: Create Mutual Benefit **117**

8. Love Work, Get a Life **123**

Improve your life balance 123
Health and wellbeing 126
Taking time to reflect 127
Companies that use mindfulness 131
Be productive not busy 133
Is it time for a four-day week? 135
Shorter working day or working week 139

Case Study: W. L. Gore **140**

9. Select Managers Who Are Good at Managing **144**

The role of the manager 147
Listen 151
The role is to coach 152

Let people choose their managers 155
Two tracks of promotion 157
Elect your leaders 160

Case Study: Basecamp **161**

10. Play to Your Strengths 164

Case Study: Netflix **167**

11. Self-Managing Organisations 173

12. The Evidence for Happy Workplaces 177

Happy workplaces are more profitable 179
Happy workplaces have lower costs 180
Happy workplaces, more share growth 182
Happy workplaces in the public sector 183
More benefits of happy workplaces 184
Happy people live longer and lead more fulfilling lives 186
The benefits of gratitude 187

Bibliography and Sources 188

Bibliography 188
Blogs and podcasts 193

Index 194

How to Contact Happy 201
Notes 202

Foreword

Can you remember your first encounter with the world of work?

Mine happened in the late 1970s: a summer working in the circulation department of a local newspaper. The office I was assigned to was deep in the bowels of the building. Delivery vans came and went, piles of newspapers were loaded. The office was dingy, smoky and routinely full of people who should have been elsewhere in the building but fancied five minutes having a chat and a cup of tea.

They were funny, friendly and introduced me to the rules of work, 1970s style: don't start work until it is exactly time to do so; stop work at precisely clocking-off time; distrust all managers; do what you are supposed to do and no more; never volunteer. I had a two-page job description for the most menial of jobs.

In the workplaces of the 20th century there was little room for, or understanding of, employee engagement. Brilliant people left their intelligence, energy and enthusiasm at the door.

There was certainly no joy.

Depressingly and amazingly, in too many 21st-century organisations these things still hold true.

It does not have to be this way.

Treating people well – as they want to be treated – and giving them the freedom and space to express their brilliance is the way forward. It simply has to be.

Recent research by Salesforce concludes that the employee experience drives revenues and profits and that companies routinely miss out on 50 per cent of the growth available by neglecting the employee experience. The amazing thing is that research is required to prove this. Happy employees look after customers better and help create prosperous organisations.

Pioneers like Henry Stewart prove that joy at work is not a contradiction in terms, but essential to create humane *and* high-performing organisations. People are infinitely more important than profit, but the two can co-exist, indeed they must do so to create sustainable organisations.

The work of Henry and Happy is not an interesting experiment on the margins of organisational life. It is much more important and mainstream than that. It provides an inspirational route to re-shaping organisations and how they are managed. And it is practical. It works. Joy works! Clearly and irresistibly, this book explains how.

Stuart Crainer
Co-founder, Thinkers50

Introduction

> "Happiness and contentment at work is not about sushi for lunch and massages at your desk, it is about how bosses treat those that work for them."
>
> Professor Cary Cooper

My colleague Cathy Busani decided that she wanted people at Happy to find joy in at least 80% of what they do at work. And yes, we measure it. It was initially 73% but it has now got up to 87%.

If you want to find out how to achieve that, then this book is for you. As it says on the cover, there are over 501 ideas on how to create joy at work, based on the principles of my previous book, *The Happy Manifesto*.

As it says:

> Imagine a workplace where people are energised and motivated by being in control of the work they do. Imagine they are trusted and given freedom, within clear guidelines, to decide how to achieve their results. Imagine they are able to get the life balance they want. Imagine they are valued according to the work that they do, rather than the number of hours they spend at their desk. Wouldn't you want to work there?

If that is the sort of workplace you want to create, then you will find lots of great ideas here.

At Happy we seek to create joy at work, for ourselves and for our clients. Generally, we see this as about creating a culture based on trust and freedom, and creating environments where people enjoy coming to work and can feel fulfilled.

Some of the ideas here are from organisations that have specifically sought to apply the ideas in *The Happy Manifesto*, some are from Happy and some are taken from other sources.

What I've found since the Manifesto's publication is that people love the ideas and really value reading about the practical steps that companies have taken, "nickables" that you can put into practice in your organisation. This playbook is packed with such ideas. Feel free to pinch with pride.

This book is based on the ten principles of *The Happy Manifesto*, together with eleven case studies of organisations that, in one way or another, follow these ideas.

This is a work in progress. If you have examples from your own experience, please do send them to me at henry@happy.co.uk. I really value hearing about other people's ideas for a joyful workplace.

Enjoy!

Who is Happy?

Happy is a London-based learning provider that helps organisations create happy, productive workplaces, based on trust and freedom.

Check out our courses and programmes at www.happy.co.uk

The Happy Manifesto: 10 Principles for a Great Workplace

These are the simple ideas that can change workplaces and make them great places to be, and more productive too.

1. Trust your people
Step out of approval. Instead pre-approve and focus on supporting your people.

2. Make your people feel good
Make this the focus of management, building confidence in your people.

3. Give freedom within clear guidelines
People want to know what is expected of them. But they want freedom to find the best way to achieve their goals.

4. Be open and transparent
More information means people can take responsibility and ownership, and brings inclusivity.

5. Recruit for attitude, train for skill
Instead of qualifications and experience, recruit on attitude and potential ability.

6. Celebrate mistakes
Create a truly no-blame culture, to enable people to innovate without fear

7. Community: create mutual benefit
Have a positive impact on the world and build your organisation too.

8. Love work, get a life
The world, and your job, needs you well rested, well nourished and well supported.

9. Select managers who are good at managing
Make sure your people are supported by somebody who is good at doing that, and find other routes for those whose strengths are elsewhere. Even better, allow people to choose their managers.

10. Play to your strengths
Make sure your people spend most of their time doing what they are best at.

Case Study: Happy

Happy helps organisations create happy, productive workplaces. We do this through a mixture of delivering learning and consultancy. It is important to us that we model what we are trying to create, based on the principles in *The Happy Manifesto*.

Happy was established in 1987 as Happy Computers, which sought to make learning about software a fun, enjoyable and productive process. I started the company after working in a deeply unhappy workplace, which brought me to the edge of a nervous breakdown.

I wanted to find out how you created a company that was principled, effective, delivered great service to its customers and was a good place to work.

The key turning point in that long journey was in 1992, when I read *Maverick* by Ricardo Semler. That told the story of how he turned his father's factory into a workplace based entirely on trust. (See the case study on Semco, further on in the book.)

It was a revelation and was the basis for everything that has followed at Happy.

Create Joy at Work

The aim at Happy is for every person to find joy in their work at least 80% of the time. And we measure it (at the four-monthly check-ins). Our latest figure is an average of 87%.

1. **Play to people's strengths:** A key element in finding that joy is, we find, doing stuff you are good at. At Happy, we recruit to a job description and then throw it away. Instead we have team job descriptions. Each of our people is encouraged to think about what they are, or have the potential to be, good at and how they can do more of it.

2. **Managers as coaches:** Our "managers" used to be called co-ordinators and, after a staff vote, are now called M&Ms

(mentors and multipliers). It is very clearly understood that their role is not to tell people what to do, or demonstrate their expertise, but to coach and help people find their own solutions.

> "I love my sessions with Cathy. I always leave my one-to-ones more excited and inspired than when I went in."
>
> Lydia Theaker

3.   **Separate the roles of managers:** At Happy we have five heads of department. Some are also M&Ms, coaching their people. Some are not. The role of thinking through the needs of that department is separated from the role of supporting, challenging and coaching people.

4.   **Choose your manager:** New starters are allocated an M&M. After three months, however, they can choose whoever they want to be their manager, remembering that the role of a manager is to coach.

5.   **Transparency in action:** Everything from the company finances to individual salaries are available internally at Happy. We do everything we can, including using Lego™, to help people understand those finances. And all our people can look up everybody's salary (now and at every stage since they joined the company) in a simple spreadsheet.

6.   **Trust people:** The aim is that everybody is trusted to make decisions in their area, within whatever guidelines are appropriate. Everybody feels pre-approved, as long as they work within Happy's values.

7.   **Senior leadership makes no decisions:** Based on the ideas of David Marquet (as described later), from 2017 the senior leadership team at Happy decided to make no decisions, but to create the environment for others to step up, normally those closest to the decision point. Happy was at that point flatlining in terms of sales. In the two years afterwards sales grew by 25% a year, based on people taking real accountability.

8. **Celebrate mistakes:** I know that one of the things people appreciate at Happy is the fact that if they take a risk, try something new, and it goes wrong, we will celebrate the mistake.

9. **Recruit for attitude:** We never ask for qualifications, avoid CVs and seek to recruit for attitude. In the interview, as far as possible, we get people to do the job they have applied for. We seek to hire collaboratively, involving everybody who will be working with them.

We recruit our facilitators - the coaches who train people from other companies - in groups of six at a time, so we can see how they interact and whether they are positive and supportive of each other. We make sure they are clear on what is needed and then ask them to train each other.

While we throw in one or two challenges (such as taking them aside in the 2nd interview to be coached, and then seeing if they change), we do not at any point ask them any questions.

Overall, our aim is to create a fulfilling workplace where people are trusted and can work at their best.

1. Trust Your People

Our experience is that people work best when they are trusted and given freedom, within guidelines, to use their own judgement. How do you, as a manager, step away from approval and instead give your people the ability to make their own decisions?

Trust-based workplaces

A key question for most organisations is, 'how easy is it to get stuff done?' If people have to go through many levels of approval to do their job, then your organisation is not effective and people will not be fulfilled.

10. **No approval needed at Netflix:** Jennifer Nierva describes how at her previous job, at Hewlett-Packard, she had to get 20 levels of approval to employ consultants on a $200,000 contract. It took her six weeks and endless frustrating phone calls.

Joining Netflix, she came up with a $1 million marketing proposal and asked her boss who she had to get to sign it off. "Nobody," was the answer. "Just sign it and send it back." [No Rules Rules, Reed Hastings, Erin Meyer]

> "At most companies, the boss is there to approve or block the decisions of employees. This is a surefire way to limit innovation and slow down growth. When the boss steps out of the role of 'decision approver', the entire business speeds up and innovation increases."
>
> Reed Hastings, Founder, Netflix

11. **Customer service is about trust:** "The secret behind great customer service: trust your employees to serve the customers the way they want to," explained Timpson founder John Timpson. Timpson has two rules: dress the part, and put the money in the till. After that it is up to each branch to decide how to operate.

12. **Set up systems to make it inevitable that people do the right thing:** "Stop putting blocks in people's way, instead make it easy, inevitable that they do what's right. Allow people to be people," says Donna Reeves, ex-Director, Kingfisher plc.

13. **Nelson's empowered navy:** In the 1800s, the French and Spanish navies were based on orders from a central command: "by tradition, commanders of individual ships awaited orders transmitted in flag signals."

In contrast, "Nelson crafted an organizational culture that rewarded individual initiative and critical thinking, as opposed to simple execution of commands." At the Battle of Trafalgar he sent his ships to disrupt the enemy lines, knowing his commanders would be able to act on the spot, while the other side waited for orders. Britain lost none of its 27 ships but destroyed 19 of the enemy's 33 ships. [Team of Teams, Stanley McChrystal]

14. **Get rid of the Quality Improvement Team:** Ulysses Lyons, Principal at Nuneaton Sixth Form College, explained how they had moved to "doing with" rather than "doing to", having full stakeholder engagement in innovation, rather than a separate team that takes responsibility for quality: "Doing away with the quality improvement team is the best way to improve quality."

> "People's happiness in their work is not about gourmet salads or sleeping pods or foosball tables. True and abiding happiness in work comes from being deeply engaged in solving a problem with talented people you know are also deeply engaged in solving it, and from knowing that the customer loves the product or service you all have worked so hard to make."
> *Powerful*, Patty McCord, Chief Talent Officer, Netflix

15. **No scripts, trust your people:** For Zappos, the online shoe retailer bought by Amazon for a billion dollars, the focus is on trust: "When customers call us, instead of giving our employees

scripts to read, we believe that trusting our employees and giving them the freedom to do whatever it takes to make our customers happy ultimately will result in happier customers," explained Tony Hsieh, CEO of Zappos.

16. **Check it's above the waterline:** At W. L. Gore there is a concept of above the waterline and below the waterline. "Everyone at Gore consults with other knowledgeable Associates before taking actions that might be 'below the waterline', causing serious damage to the enterprise." [*Brave New Work*, Aaron Dignan]

17. **Freedom at Facebook:** "At any given point in time, there isn't just one version of Facebook running, there are probably ten thousand," explained Mark Zuckerberg in the podcast 'Facebook 10,000 Versions'.[1] "Any engineer at the company can basically decide that they want to test something. There are some rules on sensitive things, but in general, an engineer can test something, and they can launch a version of Facebook not to the whole community, but maybe to 10,000 people or 50,000 people – whatever is necessary to get a good test of an experience.

"And then, they get a readout of how that affected all of the different metrics, and things that we care about. How were people connecting? How were people sharing? Do people have more friends in this version? Of course, business metrics, like how does this cost the efficiency of running the service, how much revenue are we making?"

18. **Remove the locks:** In an example still remembered at Hewlett-Packard, in the early days Bill Hewlett took a bolt cutter to a lock on a supply room door to signify the importance of trust and openness between management and frontline staff. [*CEO Excellence*, Carolyn Dewar, Scott Keller and Vikram Malhotra]

19. **Let your people decide:** When Jan Carlzon took over the SAS airline in 1981, it was struggling. Within a year it was the most punctual airline in Europe and made a $54 million profit.

Key to its success was decentralisation. Jan "gave his frontline staff the power to solve customer service problems on the spot, without having to check with their supervisors first. This greatly improved customer satisfaction, employee morale, and corporate profit ... a win-win situation for all involved." [The Like Switch, Jack Schafer]

20. **The 98%:** Set rules for the 98% trying to do a good job, not the 2% that aren't.

> "The knowledge worker cannot be supervised closely or in detail. He must direct himself."
> Peter Drucker, 1967

Pre-approval

It is common to ask people to solve a problem, or come up with an improvement to a service, and bring it back for approval. The concept of pre-approval is that you miss out that last step. As the manager you approve the solution before your people have come up with a solution. Instead you agree clear guidelines (budget, requirements, metrics, who they should talk to) and leave them to implement a solution.

21. **Pre-approval for the new website at TLC (Talk, Listen, Change):** "One of our key elements over the last couple of years has been freedom within clear guidelines. We very much use pre-approval. We did some work at the beginning about working out what the brand guidelines were and what being Brand Guardian meant, and then we've said, 'off you go, it's up to you, you're our marketing expert'.

"Some of the differences that we've seen in how we've built a brand are just amazing. Our new website launched about six weeks ago. The first day I saw the website was the day after it launched. The first few weeks Paige was asking me, 'what do you think about this colour, what do you think about this font', but I reminded her to go back to what we said about pre-approval. She knew the outcome we were aiming for. You almost saw her come to life, because actually she's really creative, she thinks really quickly, she wants to test new things, and actually the website is amazing. The difference that we've seen in traffic through to the website in the last month is unbelievable." Michelle Hill, CEO, TLC (Talk, Listen, Change) at the 2017 Happy Workplaces Conference.

22. **Get your most junior staff to make the key decisions:** GCHQ, one of the UK's intelligence agencies, needs to be at the forefront of technology. So a group of staff secured a £1 million budget for innovation from their directors. They set up a crowdsourcing site, OneShot, where staff could post a request. It might be £500 for this idea, for example, or £8,000 for that piece of technology.

In most companies, the decision on who got the money would be made by senior managers or directors. At GCHQ they split the £1 million into 100 sets of £10,000 and gave that amount to the most junior members of staff to decide how it was allocated.

One person explained how they had an idea for a piece of technology that would vastly improve communications, but would cost £10,000. Previously it might have required five levels of approval and they probably wouldn't have bothered. But they put it up on OneShot, it was fully funded within a week and implemented within two weeks. The effect was to hugely increase the speed of decision-making, but also to change who made the decisions. Now it was people closer to the front line.

23. **$2,000 without approval to please a guest:** At hotel group Ritz Carlton employees can spend up to $2,000 to satisfy a guest or deal with any issues, without needing approval. [Team of Teams, Stanley McChrystal]

24. **Give your staff power, and £500, to resolve issues:** At Timpson staff are expected to use their judgement in dealing with any problems and can spend up to £500 to settle a complaint. "It has saved us a fortune," explained founder John Timpson.

25. **Staff can spend £250 without checking:** At SocialAdventures, Chief Executive Scott Darrugh describes how managers got frustrated with having to approve minor spending, and with basic maintenance not getting done. So they said anybody could spend up to £250 on anything they felt was needed.

"Not only did it free up management time, and make sure problems got fixed quickly," explains Scott, "but it also led to a 6% fall in spending."

26. **Improving your people's work takes away the ownership:** A director at the UK's National Audit Office explained when he understood about "improving" work: "A decade ago I took a report from my team and spent two days transforming it. When I gave it back, the team manager came to me and said, 'What you

have produced is undoubtedly a better report. However you have completely taken away the ownership from my team and demotivated them.' It made me realise I had to find a different way to get that result."

27. **Pre-approval in a local authority:** Previously decisions on funding for block-purchased placements and respite for adults with mental health, autism or a learning disability needed to go to a forum for approval. This is a lengthy and time-consuming process.

Helen Taylor (from the London Borough of Hounslow) delegated authority to her team managers to make placement decisions about block placements and respite without a need for a panel or, indeed her intervention, to a cost of up to £100k per annum. Helen keeps this under review (as she is required to do), and to date, has not come across a single decision she would consider misplaced.

28. **Pre-approval for Carer's Week:** Nicky Bartholomew of the London Borough of Hounslow pre-approved her team to plan, budget and communicate the borough's contribution to National Carer's Week , a major national event.

Previously, Nicky checked and approved all plans, budgets, publicity, etc. and described herself as a bottleneck leading to unnecessary delays. The team have stepped up and delivered a really good event.

29. **Set high expectations but don't check the detail:** "When I was at McKinsey & Company, I had a manager named Andrew who expected perfection in the market analyses I prepared for clients. But he didn't micromanage me by telling me how to write each page or how to do my analyses. Andrew set our expectations higher. In 1999 we were serving a financial services company and doing one of the first e-commerce projects our firm had ever done.

"I brought a draft report to him and instead of editing it, he asked, 'Do I need to review this?' I knew deep down that while my report was good, he would surely find some room for improvement. Realizing this, I told him it wasn't ready and went back to refine it further. I came back to him a second time, and a second time he asked, 'Do I need to review this?' I went away again. On my fourth try, he asked the same question and I told him, 'No. You don't need to review it. It's ready for the client.' He answered, 'Terrific. Nice work.' And sent it to the client without even glancing at it." [Work Rules, Laszlo Bock]

30. **Spend what's needed at Netflix:** Nigel Baptiste, Director of Partner Engagement at Netflix, was due to demonstrate the latest Samsung TV to a *Washington Post* tech journalist. He arrived to find the TV had been disposed of along with other TVs they'd asked Facilities to get rid of. He tried calling suppliers and none had that particular TV.

Then Nick, the most junior engineer on the team, sprinted into the office. "Don't worry, Nigel," Nick said. "I solved that. I came in last night, and I saw the TV had been got rid of. You didn't respond to my calls and texts. So I drove out to the Best Buy in Tracy, bought the same TV, and tested it this morning. It cost $2,500, but I thought it was the right thing to do."

As Reed Hastings points out, Nick had used five words to guide his actions: "Act in Netflix's best interests" [No Rules Rules, Reed Hastings, Erin Meyer]

31. **Pre-approval on maternity pay:** Rackspace's purpose is "fanatical support". But Dom Monkhouse explains that some of his female staff pointed out that the maternity pay was the statutory minimum, and certainly not "fanatical".

He told them they were right and to investigate what "best in class" looks like for maternity leave. "I promised them that whatever they proposed I would accept." They "came up with an outstanding proposal, and stayed on as happy employees", many of whom are still at Rackspace. [Mind Your F**king Business, Dom Monkhouse]

32. **Don't check with the boss:** John explains: "When I started at Happy, I would email Henry – the founder – with every bit of expenditure. He soon wrote back: 'John, if it's under £400 and you think we need it, buy it. If it's over £400, check with someone, but no need to check with me.'"

33. **Pre-approval in the US Army in World War II**: President Eisenhower recalls George Marshall telling him: "[The War Department] is filled with able men who analyse the problems well but feel compelled always to bring them to me for the final solution. I must have assistants who will solve their own problems and tell me later what they have done." [A World Without Email, Cal Newport]

34. **Give your salespeople a personal advertising budget:** "Last year we gave our sellers a marketing fund for the first time", explained Jason Vallejos, Executive Vice President at Syndicated Insurance. "Most agents used the budget to meet groups of prospective customers and hold lunch-and-learns to existing ones. Online ads did well too.

"It was our best year ever. We grew by 282%." [HBR, July 2023]

So often, people get to prepare a proposal for their boss so that their boss, who hasn't done any research on the subject, can make it "better". I tell people, "Your proposal is pre-approved. You did the investigation, so I won't try to make it better."
>Dom Monkhouse, *Mind Your F**king Business*

Involve your people

If you involve your people in key decisions, you are likely to make a better decision. But, more importantly, your people are going to be more engaged in making that decision work.

35. **Vote on key decisions:** The 55,000 strong healthcare company DaVita puts democracy into practice by having staff vote on important decisions. This included the name of the company and the seven core values.

"My job as a leader here is to create an environment where our teammates can step up as leaders and make good decisions," says David Hoerman, Chief Wisdom Office, in (DaVita: a 65,000 Person Corporate Village, or Just a CEO's Nutty Dream?)[2]

36. **Let them work it out:** "One manager runs a programme in three towns that needs 12 participants in order to be viable. He had told the staff this several times and each time it ran there were less than 12 young people on it. After hearing you speak he took along all the financial information and let the team work out for themselves what was needed for the programme to go ahead and cover its costs.

"The answer was 12 participants! But there was a different result, because the staff had reached that conclusion. Each programme now has more than 12 young people on it, the young people are benefiting, and we have a happy commissioner who will continue to buy the programme!" Katherine Horler, Chief Executive, Adviza

37. **Hand your strategy to your people:** "When developing our strategy at the Stroke Association, instead of the conventional top-down process, our executive team handed this responsibility over to the organisation, inviting anyone with an interest to put themselves forward to develop the strategy.

"From an enthusiastic response, a diverse group of 12 relatively inexperienced people was selected and, with the whole organisation behind them and interacting with them, and with expert coaching support, [they] did a wonderful job of coming up with five fantastic strategic principles that continue to be our organisation's guiding light." Chris MacQueen, Associate Director Strategy and Planning, Stroke Association

38.   **Think like business innovators:** Gary Hamel describes a "mid-Western US manufacturing company" where "over the course of a year, more than 30,000 employees, many of them blue-collar union members, were taught how to think like business innovators. Out of this effort came thousands of game-changing ideas.

In one memorable, though not unusual, case a long-tenured assembly line worker hatched an idea that ultimately produced a multi-million-dollar payoff. For the first time in her career, this woman had been asked to think big, and when the chance came, she grabbed it." [Humanocracy, Gary Hamel]

Encouraging and supporting employees to think 'BIG' leads to ideas that can change everything

39.   **Let your salespeople decide how much time to spend on the phone:** Dom Monkhouse explains that his best salesperson at Rackspace spent four hours on the phone, but the rest of the team was averaging less than two hours. Instead of telling the others to spend more time, Dom asked "what do you think is the minimum amount of phone time a Rackspace salesperson should complete each day in order to do their job?"

After a team huddle, they agree three hours as a minimum. "We displayed the scores in real time on a big monitor. The results: Productivity went up. Sales went up. Efficiency spiked dramatically." [Mind Your F**king Business, Dom Monkhouse]

40.   **Let teams set the shift pattern:** Advanced Technology Services (ATS) maintains equipment in factories belonging to other companies. Seeking to reduce the time the equipment was out of

action, Site Manager Damien O'Neill consulted the customer. He thought hard about the business implications and discussed with the team before coming up with the best and fairest solution he could think of to change the working pattern for his team and improve the service.

The new shift pattern did not go down well. Within a few days several of his team told him they might have to leave. He started to hear rumours of arguments at home over the impact of the new shift patterns. Despite his best efforts the team were not happy.

Damien stepped back, remembering what he had learnt about involving teams and handing over power to them for the biggest decisions that affected them. He took a bold move. He called the team together, admitted he had got it wrong and asked them to come up with their own solution.

The team went away and came back with a completely new shift pattern where each person only worked a four-day week but where the equipment could be serviced 18 hours a day every day in line with the running of the factory. This new solution saved the client £11,000 per year.

The team completely bought into their own solution, they were happy with it and motivated to make it work. The union agreed the changes instantly since it had been suggested by its members.

41. **Get your people to design the rotas:** At United Utilities (a water and sewerage company in the north-west of England) the Customer Services Director wanted to change the call centre from nine to five on weekdays to around-the-clock. She asked the front-line staff to design the new work patterns:

"The people, my people, designed the work patterns. I have 'working grandparent' work patterns, I have 'I go out every Friday night and get absolutely trollied so don't ask me to work a Friday night but I will work any other night that you want me to work' work patterns. I am a heavily trade unionised business. I have nearly 80% trade union representation. It went straight through. Why? Because the employees had designed the work patterns.

They weren't just new work patterns, they were extended opening hours." Louise Beardmore, Customer Services Director, United Utilities

As a manager, make few or no decisions

The traditional approach is for the manager or leader to be seen as the expert, able to make the best decisions. The alternative is to coach your people, who are closer to where the decision will be implemented, to find their own solution. The role of the manager is no longer to show how clever you are, but instead to show how clever your people are.

> "Your job as a leader is not to be the smartest person in the room. It is to maximise the potential of your team." Liz Wiseman

42. **Commit to making no decisions, but with an exception:** When David Marquet was made Commander of the Sante Fe submarine, he realised he had been trained for a different model of submarine and didn't know how this one worked. That was the impetus for him deciding to make no decisions, but instead to coach his staff to make all decisions. There was one exception: if missiles were to be launched, that would still fall to him.

This was based on ensuring there was competence and clarity of intent. The result was that the Sante Fe moved from being underperforming to being the best performing submarine in US Navy history. Eleven of the crew themselves later became commanders of submarines. "And all this with a Captain who was a dummy and made no decisions," commented David Marquet in his excellent animated video.[3]

43. **Beware of HIPPOs:** This is a Google slogan: Beware of the Highest Paid Person's Opinion. The person who is most senior is too often the person who gets listened to in meetings.

However they are often the person most distant from the

Be aware of the HIPPO in the room (Highest Paid Persons Opinion) - give an equal voice to front line staff

front line and from the customer. Instead, give those who are on the front line an equal voice in the decisions.

Are you the HIPPO in your organisation, and are you the person who dominates in meetings?

44. **Get the boss to make no decisions:** "At B&Q we got two store managers to agree to make no decisions for three months. Instead they would coach their staff to decide for themselves. Over that period every KPI [Key Performance Indicator] improved in those stores, and staff could respond immediately to customers.

"As one said, 'The shackles have been removed. We can now say to a customer, "Yes, I can do that for you".'" Donna Reeves, ex-Director, Kingfisher plc

45. **Be the boss just one day a week:** When Alison Kriel was headteacher of Northwold Primary School in Hackney she only acted as headteacher one day in six. Each member of her management team (the deputies and the key stage heads) took on the role of head of the school for a day in a rota. "It certainly made succession planning easier," Alison commented.

46. **Avoid decisions:** "We are seeking to avoid top level decisions. Take the staff conference: the team organised this themselves, I just turned up on the day. It was within budget and a fabulous day." Katherine Horler, Chief Executive, Adviza

47. **No decisions for CEO:** Kevin Rogers, Chief Executive of Paycare (a health cash plan provider in Wolverhampton) took up the Happy challenge of making no decisions for a quarter, from Jan 2019. "It was our best quarter in more than ten years. I decided to continue doing it and ask the next level of Directors to try it too."

48. **No budgets:** "At Mayden we work without expenditure budgets. For twenty years we have worked on the basis that people spend what is needed." Chris May, founder, Mayden

> "I rarely attend meetings and almost never make decisions. We recently had a cocktail party to

celebrate the 10-year anniversary since I last made a decision."

Ricardo Semler, CEO Semco, *Maverick*

49.   **Let staff decide their own expenses:** In a very interesting experiment at the pharma multi-national Roche, two groups of staff – in Germany and Switzerland – were told that their travel claims were to become self-authorised.

Instead of being approved in advance and signed off afterwards, each employee would decide for themselves what was needed (though still aware of company policy). Instead of being checked, the resulting expenses would be displayed on the intranet. 45% of participants said their motivation had increased from being trusted in this way (against 6% feeling uncomfortable with the approach), and 75% said it was more efficient and took less time. [Becoming a Better Boss, Julian Birkinshaw]

50.   **Avoid top-down:** "I learned that the old top-down approach to management – having a few smart executives first formulate a strategy and its implementation plan, then tell everybody else in the company what to do while crafting incentives to motivate them – rarely works." [The Heart of Business, Hubert Joly]

> Vala Afshar, Chief Digital Evangelist at Salesforce, tweeted "You likely have to get management approval for a $500 expense … but you can call a 1 hour meeting with 20 people and no one notices."

The Advice Process

The Advice Process is based on individuals taking responsibility, rather than seeking consensus. Corporate Rebels[4] explains it like this:

1. Someone notices a problem or opportunity and takes the initiative, or alerts someone better placed to do so.
2. Prior to a proposal, the decision-maker may seek input to gather perspectives before proposing action.
3. The initiator makes a proposal and seeks advice from those affected or those with expertise.
4. Taking this advice into account, the decision-maker decides on an action and informs those who have given advice.

Usually, the decision-maker is the person whose area is most affected, or who initiated an idea, or discovered a problem, or saw an opportunity.

51. **Changing prices at Happy:** Two colleagues, John and Ben, decided our pricing was out of date. They analysed the market, found out what competitors were charging and consulted colleagues. But the decision was made neither by consensus nor consent. After seeking advice, John and Ben decided on the new pricing model. It represented substantial increases. (I told them I didn't agree. However, it was not my decision to make.) The new pricing was put in place.

I have to admit I was probably wrong. Thirty years after founding Happy, I was too wedded to our old models. Indeed, without that increase, and its impact on our bank balance, we might not have survived the pandemic.

52. **Under £6k, make your own decision:** Equal Experts makes extensive use of the Advice Process. "If the spend is under £6,000, it's a personal decision. Between £6,000 and £20,000, the decision falls to the business unit lead to confirm the decision maker. If it impacts multiple business units or it's above £20,000, then

someone on the executive team confirms who becomes the decision maker." An alternative to the business lead would be to use consent decision making, below.) [Lead Together; Brent Lowe, Susan Basterfield, Travis Marsh]

53. **Consent decision-making:** This is a great way to get advice, while leaving responsibility with the individual. Consensus decision-making requires people to say "Yes". Consent decision-making just requires them not to say "No". Here's how it works:

- The individual creates a proposal (often after already having sought advice).

- Colleagues ask clarifying questions.

- The proposer addresses the questions. They may decide to change the proposal, or even to take it away to come back later.

- People are then asked if anybody has any objection (key point: is it safe enough to try?)

> "Make sure that all members of the organization can make any decision, as long as they consult with the people affected and the people who have expertise on the matter."
> Frederick Laloux in *Reinventing Organisations*.

Trade unions are your friends

Many businesses, such as Amazon and Starbucks, regard trade unions as the enemy. Some more enlightened companies see trade unions as people to work with to create a better result.

54. **Southwest Airlines, profitable every year for 40 years, is 82% unionised:** Founder Herb Kelleher's people-based philosophy extended to treating the unions as partners. A US trade union website[5] notes that Southwest has "the best relationship with its unions, and the highest customer satisfaction ratings". In 2008 the Transport Workers Union made Herb an honorary lifetime member "in grateful appreciation for [his] unparalleled leadership in creating a magnificent airline and a generation of employees who love coming to work".

55. **Invite union reps (or staff representatives) to all senior management meetings:** Paul Wakeling, Principal at Havering Sixth Form College, explained how it took a lot of support and work to put this into practice, but he feels it has paid off in terms of more inclusiveness and better decisions. "Especially when you say something you think is uncontroversial and you see a reaction. And you know, if you'd gone ahead, that would have been the reaction of people across the organisation."

56. **Leave open seats at your executive meetings:** Learning from Paul's example at Havering, we decided to leave two seats open to staff on a first-come, first-served basis. Anybody can now attend the Happy Senior Leadership Team meeting, which takes place for half an hour, once a month.

As my colleague Laura explains, "I get insight into the whole picture across the company, not just what happens in my team."

Setting salaries in a trust-based workplace

Could salaries be based on a democratic process? Many organisations do enable that.

57. **Decide salaries at a panel:** At Happy we have a salary panel of four and all are elected by our staff. People put their case for an increase and the panel decides.

58. **The salary pot is decided by Happy staff:** The employees also decide the size of the salary pot. We have always had transparent finances and so I explain what the income and profit was last year, and what the projection is for this year.

People then discuss what they think the size of the pot should be, and then answer a one-question survey. The median figure is chosen.

59. **Let staff decide the approach:** "We have set up a working group of staff to evaluate what enables somebody to progress and what the salary policy should be." Katharine Horler, CEO, Adviza

60. **Let the money gang decide:** At Brighton-based Nixon McInnes a committee made up of board members and those elected by staff approved all salary decisions. Employees submitted their own proposals and the "money gang" decide if it was fair and affordable. [Worldblu, 50 transformational practices]

61. **Let your people choose the CEO salary:** At Happy we, as of 2021, let the staff decide my salary as head of the company (actually our Chief Happiness Officer). I presented my case, and how much I was requesting, and the employees filled in a two-question survey to state the rise they proposed.

In the first year I proposed a rise of 4.2%, on top of inflation. Overall the response was an offer of 5%, with one person saying "I'd double that" and another proposing three times that amount. I have to say I felt very valued by the responses.

62.   **At Haier, colleagues decide your salary:** This avoids the trap of having managers decide what you get. Instead colleagues rate you on a five-star scale. Three stars will get a salary that conforms to the market. Four or five stars will get you a bigger reward. If you get only two stars or less, your salary could be cut. "This sense of fair play is engraved in Haier's culture; people are judged on their ability, not on their working relationship with people in the right places, or their negotiation skills at interview." [Start-Up Factory, Joost Minaar, Pim de Morree, Bran van der Lecq]

63.   **Train your people in financials and then let them set their own salaries:** Pim de Morree, of Corporate Rebels, described a Dutch IT company who employ about 300 people. The first step was to open up the salary levels to everyone in the company to show they were fair. If they were not fair in the opinion of the employees, they had to think of a solution.

First they trained them in the basic financials and then they involved them in setting their own salaries to become entrepreneurs, more than just simply employees. They did this in teams. Most people did not raise their salaries higher than the normal pay rises, and they actually set their salary increases lower than management would normally have done.

64.   **Merit Money:**   At Brazilian company *Fonte Medicina Diagnóstica,* Cláudio Pires came up with the idea of, on top of their salary, giving every member of staff the same bonus.

However they have to give the bonus away, to other staff. You can give it to the same person, or spread it in small amounts. As *Vasco Duarte explains*: "People just know 'good' behaviour will pay off. Dysfunctional behaviour will be 'dealt' with: you won't get any money."

Case Study: Buurtzorg

Imagine a company with 15,000 staff and no managers. Imagine annual sales of over 300 million euros and no Chief Financial Officer, with only six people working in finance. Imagine it has grown to that size from, back in 2006, having just four staff – although it is not-for-profit and has no venture capital investment.

The organisation is Buurtzorg, which, over those years, has grown from nothing to provide over two-thirds of Dutch community nursing care. Without those layers of management, it is uniquely focused on the front-line staff, the nurses, and on the needs of the patients.

65. **No management meetings:** "We have not had one management meeting since we started," explains Jos de Blok, the co-founder. "In my former job we had a lot of meetings that were only about meetings. Now we just have time to solve the problems."

The Buurtzorg model is based on traditional Dutch care, with nurses based in local communities. In the 1980s and 1990s this approach was changed to introduce the "efficiency" of modern management methods. Centralised call centres took the calls from patients and central planners would allocate the jobs to nurses, and stipulate the time to spend with each person. A patient might see dozens of different nurses over a year, and have to explain their problems to each one.

66. **A nurse-led approach:** Buurtzorg has returned to a nurse-led approach. There are no call centres. Nurses take the calls. Where elsewhere head-office planners decide who visits whom, nurses – in self-managing teams of ten to twelve nurses – plan patient visits and decide how long they should spend there, depending on their judgement of the need.

With only 45 people in the head office, overhead costs are 8% instead of the 25% that is standard in the industry.

67. **Vocation:** With nurses able to fulfil their vocation and respond according to their judgement, staff satisfaction is high and sickness among staff is a little over half that of other care companies. And Buurtzorg is consistently top for patient satisfaction, out of over 300 Dutch nursing providers.

For Jos de Blok, there are three simple principles behind the success:
1. Do what's needed.
2. Reflect on what you are doing, and try to do it better.
3. Use your common sense, or "common sensing" as Jos puts it.

"Let's avoid complexity. Even with 15,000 people, it can be a very simple organisation. We must build organisations based on meaningful relationships. When nurses feel happy they will stay healthy and they will do good things," explained Jos de Blok.

68. **Total focus on the patient need:** A group of nurses within the organisation had noticed that when their elderly patients suffered a fall, they often broke their hips, which reduced their autonomy (sometimes permanently). So they created a new programme focused on accident prevention and delivered it in their local market. They were so excited with the results that they brought them to Buurtzorg CEO Jos de Blok.

Sometimes it's better to share the story and process to inspire change rather than rolling it out

This programme should be rolled out across the entire company, they said. But instead of assigning a task force, or piloting the programme in other regions, or announcing it as a company-wide initiative, he did something else entirely. He asked the team to write a story about what they'd created and publish it to the company's internal social network, along with a guidebook for how to set up the programme. If the idea was good, he reasoned, it would spread.

69. **More care for the client takes less time:** "A 2009 Ernst & Young study found that Buurtzorg requires, on average, close to 40 percent fewer hours of care per client than other nursing organisations – which is ironic when you consider that nurses in Buurtzorg take time for coffee and talk with the patients, their families and neighbours, while other nursing organisations have come to time 'products' in minutes."

Why? "Patients stay in care only half as long, heal faster, and become more autonomous." [Reinventing Organisations, Frederick Laloux]

Huge savings to the Dutch healthcare system: "A third of emergency hospital admissions are avoided, and when a patient does need to be admitted to the hospital, the average stay is shorter. The savings for the Dutch social security system are considerable – the Ernst & Young study estimated that close to €2 billion would be saved in the Netherlands every year if all home care organisations achieved Buurtzorg's results." [Reinventing organisations, Frederick Laloux]

2. Make Your People Feel Good

Nearly everybody we have asked agrees with the statement "people work best when they feel good about themselves".

If that is true, it makes sense to make that idea (creating an environment where people feel good about themselves) a focus of leadership and management.

Here's some ideas on how to do it:

> "Employees in the new workforce aren't looking for amenities such as game rooms, free food and fancy latte machines. But they are looking for benefits and perks that will improve their wellbeing – those that offer them greater flexibility, autonomy and the ability to lead a better life."
> *It's the Manager*, Jim Clifton, Jim Harper]

Build relationships

Great relationships, between peers and between leaders and employees, are crucial to a happy workplace.

> "We got lots of advice on how to scale the business but none on how to scale our relationships. Good relationships at work make you feel trusted, respected, understood, empowered, supported, appreciated, energised."
> Rosie Brown, MD, Cook

70. **Leave people feeling good:** At Happy one of our core values is to make people feel good. That means, even when it is a challenging or difficult situation, you still leave them feeling good.

That should be a key role of leaders in any organisation, but perhaps also of everybody.

71. **Take time to talk:** "Every day, take five minutes to talk to one of your employees with no other agenda. Just go up and ask how they are and what's going on." [Leading with Happiness, Alexander Kjerulf]

72. **Take breaks together to improve productivity:** MIT Professor Sandy Pentland studied interaction at a Bank of America call centre in 2008. When he shifted coffee breaks from individuals taking them on their own to being team-based, interaction rose and call times (the key measure) dropped.

When this break system was rolled out to all call centres, it resulted in $15 million saved in productivity, due to those better relationships. [Team of Teams, Stanley McChrystal]

73. **Ring five employees a week:** "We have 230 staff. Now for half an hour on a Monday morning I ring five people I don't normally see. I love it and, from the emails I get afterwards, it seems they do too." Katherine Horler, Chief Executive, Adviza

74. **Smile:** The research[6] backs up that smiling is contagious, and helps you to be happier too.

75. **Say thank you:** When I asked a friend what made them happy at work, they said "my manager. They thank me every day."

76. **It's all about relationships:** "Our sense of happiness and fulfilment across life depends on the quality of our relationships. Relationships drive business performance. We have 90 shops and the best performance comes from those with the best relationships." Rosie Brown, MD, Cook

77. **Lots of the best things are free:** "Say thank you. Show appreciation. Care for others. Help everybody feel part of the community. These are all free." Sarah Gillard, Director, John Lewis Partnership.

78. **Create a culture of "I've got your back":** "Create a culture where everybody feels that others are absolutely on their side." Derek Hill, MD, ATS

> "I will tell the story through the underlying principles that guided our turnaround: always start with people; always end with people; and generate human energy."
>
> *The Heart of Business*, Hubert Joly

79. **Have talking partners:** At Next Jump everybody has a "talking partner", who they see several times a week and share their challenges and thoughts. It is similar to a mentoring relationship, but Next Jump believes that conventional mentoring, where a senior person helps a junior member of staff, fails 95% of the time.

Talking partners is instead co-mentoring. "Partner with somebody different to you," suggests Tarun Gidoomal. "You push each other to go to the places you don't want to go."

"The idea is that your partner's success is almost more important than your own," explained Henry Searle at Happy's 2016 Happy Workplaces Conference. Henry is co-Managing Director of the London office with Tarun and also his talking partner. Both times I have heard a Next Jump speaker at a conference, they have come with their talking partner, whose role was totally supportive. Imagine having somebody in your organisation that is 100% there for you.

Having someone different to you as a "talking partner" who supports and listens to you, can help push you further

80. **Doughnut buddies:** Industrial maintenance company ATS uses the Donut feature in Slack. Every two weeks it randomly selects pairs, across the company, to meet for coffee (and, possibly, doughnuts). "It's become a real point of excitement," explained MD Derek Hill. "When it comes round, everybody is asking 'who is your buddy this time?'"

81. **Written appreciation:** "In the holiday period I write what I appreciate about each person on a star under the tree. They get to see [it] and so do their colleagues." Annie McDowall, CEO, Share Community

82. **Go for a walk:** "Building relationships doesn't need to cost a fortune. We have ideas like 'Go and have a meeting walking on the South Downs'." Rosie Brown, MD, Cook

83. **Get remote workers to meet:** "We have lot of remote workers. So we have created clusters of four or five staff who live nearby and encourage them to meet up, after a day of interviewing clients, for coffee. For some it's once a month, for some it's every week." Katherine Horler, Chief Executive, Adviza

84. **Create a "user manual for me":** Create a one-page profile of each of your people. In the organisation Wellbeing Teams, it includes "What people like about me", "What is important to me", "How to support me".

"It ensures everybody is seen as a person," explains Helen Sanderson, CEO of Wellbeing Teams. "It helps people feel valued and builds mutual support."

85. **The platinum rule:** The golden rule says treat people as you would want to be treated. The platinum rule says treat people as *they* would want to be treated.

I am great at managing people like me, expressives. However I'm not so good at managing people who are more introverted, or analytical. (Which is why I don't manage – or coach – people at Happy.)

> "Three things in human life are important. The first is to be kind. The second is to be kind. And the third is to be kind."
>
> Henry James

Joy at work

It was said that at the Ford River Rouge plant in the 1930s, you could be sacked for laughing (Google it). We believe that if you can help people create joy in their work, it can create true fulfilment.

86. **Help your people find joy at work:**
"Help them do something they are good at, working to their strengths and having the freedom to do it well. My goal is for all my team to get joy at work in 80% of what they do. I reckon I'm at 95%. Do what you love."
Cathy Busani, MD at Happy

Finding joy is about working to your strengths and doing what you are good at

At Happy we get people to measure how much of their work they find joy in, in their four-monthly snapshots. It was originally, on average, 73% but has now reached 87%.

87. **Find purpose and passion:** "Fear-based leadership leads to command and control. Freedom-based leadership leads to empowered workplaces. It's not about ping-pong and perks. It's about purpose and passion." Derek Hill, MD, ATS

> "My passionate belief is that businesses can be fun; they can be conducted with love and a powerful force for good."
> Anita Roddick, co-founder of The Body Shop, in *Compact Guide to Excellence*, Tom Peters

88. **Joy at work is the best route to quality:** When the quality team at East London Foundation Trust checked what made teams work well and deliver quality provision, they found the key factor was having joy at work. As a result, they made the key quality focus one of creating joy at work.

"My role is to help teams feel they have permission to try different things," explained Auzewell Chitewe. "It's not about what the organisation can do for them but about empowering the teams. In healthcare we have what we call wicked problems. You can't solve them doing things the way we always have. It's not about some geniuses figuring out a solution. It is about giving permission to those closest to the problem to come up with solutions, and specifically to involve the 'service user' (or patient) in that solution. They have to have the freedom to fail."

89.   **Ask "will it make us happier?":** When Ben Hunt-Davis and his team were training for the Sydney Olympics in 2000 (where they won gold in the rowing eights), the key question at all times was "will it make the boat go faster?" An extra hour training? Yes, it will make the boat go faster. A pint down the pub? No, so they didn't do it.

"So we ask 'will it make us happier?' and 'will it make life better?' If the answer is No, we don't do it." Nikki Gatenby, CEO, Propellernet

> "In that moment, I realized why my other startups had failed and why Twitter was going to work. Twitter brought me joy. I was laughing out loud on a Sunday afternoon using the application that I had spent many days and nights working on. I was passionate about this project."
> *Things a Little Bird Told Me*, Biz Stone

90.   **Employee passion:** Indian company HCL decided to survey not just employee satisfaction (for which the company was ranked no. 1 in India in 2009) but also their passion, and to share the results. People got to think about what drove them to act passionately and how they could best leverage this at work.

91.   **Give praise, not criticism:** "I have yet to find the person, however great or exalted his station, who did not do better work and put forth greater effort under a spirit of approval than he would ever do under a spirit of criticism." Charles Schwab, CEO, Bethlehem Steel, in [How to win friends and influence people, Dale Carnegie]

Happiness as a focus

Can happiness be the ultimate purpose of your business? It is for some companies.

> "The science is clear: Making other people happy makes you happier too."
>
> Arlette Bentzen, WooHoo Inc.

92. **Make happiness the "ultimate purpose" of the business:** That is what Spedan Lewis did in the 1920s when he set up the John Lewis Partnership as a workers' mutual. Every decision was to be made on how happy it made the staff. With that core focus, the company has grown from 300 staff then to 85,000 now.

When I spoke on a panel alongside Charlie Mayfield, then Chair of the John Lewis Partnership, he explained that at the last Board meeting, five hours long, they spent just 20 minutes discussing the numbers. "The rest was spent on how to motivate and develop our people."

93. **Discover the "three potatoes of workplace happiness":** Laurence Vanhee (ex-CHO, Belgian Ministry of Social Security) believes the key to happiness at work is to ensure people are doing "what I do well", "what I love" and "what is useful".

(No, I'm not sure why it's three potatoes.)

94. **Happiness at work pays:** When the Belgian Ministry of Social Security focused on happiness at work, results improved dramatically. Laurence Vanhee, Chief Happiness Officer, explained at the 2018 Happy Workplaces Conference that productivity rose by 20%, rental costs fell by 12 million euros and maintenance costs by 50%. Spontaneous applications rose by 500%. Staff turnover fell by 75%.

95. **Create a happiness plan:** "That's what the team of happiness ambassadors at Danish insurance company SEB does. Every year, just as you might have a sales plan, they create a plan of how to make SEB happier," explained Arlette Bentzen of WooHoo at the 2018 Happy Workplaces Conference.

> **Seek *arbejdsglaede*:** Only the Scandinavians have a word for work happiness, and this is it in Danish.

96. **Team Shout Out Board:** "We have a board thanking your team for anything they have done for you. We share and shout them out in our Monday morning all-team huddle meeting." Rosie Brown, MD, Cook

Fulfilling dreams

Some organisations help their people to achieve their greatest dreams.

97.   **Help your people fulfil their dreams**: "One of our people was a mad keen cyclist so, when we got interest from cycling firm Evans, he got to lead it. Another was committed to wildlife conservation in Africa. We teamed her up with a sustainable safari company in Namibia. They pay us in safaris – it's very popular with staff!" Nikki Gatenby, CEO, Propellernet

98.   **Create a Dream Academy:** "At Cook we have the Dream Academy to help our people achieve their personal dreams. Dream It. Plan it. Do It."

"Since the COOK Dream Academy started in 2013, over 100 people – members of our team and customers – have had a series of confidential one-on-one coaching sessions with our Dream Manager, Alastair Hill. Anybody can choose to do so. So far, every single one of them has recommended it." Rosie Brown, MD, Cook

99.   **Help your people fulfil their dreams**: Propellernet has a dream machine (an old bubble-gum dispenser). People put what they'd love to do in a dreamball and every so often one gets drawn. The first two went to the World Cup in Brazil. Another motorcycled round Africa. Propellernet pays for the activity. "We literally make our people's dreams come true." Nikki Gatenby, CEO, Propellernet

> "It's not rocket science. Happy people do better work than miserable people."
>
> Nikki Gatenby, Managing Director, Propellernet

100. **Have a secret "angel" for "love week":** At Malaysian company Mindvalley the aim is to make every member of staff feel valued and working in a way that aligns with their personal vision. One example is "love week",[7] where every member of staff gets a secret "angel" whose role is to make them feel loved.

101. **Wheel of fortune at WebMart:** At print company WebMart, there is a wheel of fortune on which every member of staff has one dream they'd like to do. When the company wins an award or a big sale or gets great results, they spin the wheel of fortune and somebody gets to enjoy their dream.

Material benefits

Material benefits help too. They can range from buying a holiday home for your people, right down to a £5 peer-to-peer voucher.

102. **Buy a holiday home for your staff to use:** Cook, who make "remarkable frozen ready meals", bought a holiday home in Kent at a cost of £80,000 and provide it free to staff. "It is especially popular with our lower-paid staff and it's great to be able to give people a good break," explained Alison Payne, People Director at Cook.

103. **Renovate houses to create homes for your staff:** Housing is hard to buy in Brighton, especially with the competition from people moving down from London. So search marketing agency Propellernet decided to buy up run-down properties, renovate them and sell them to staff. "This has been life-changing for some of our people and hasn't even cost us anything. We sold some of the flats on the market and actually made money from the activity." Nikki Gatenby, CEO, Propellernet

104. **Share the wealth:** John Lewis's profit share varies up to 15% of annual salary. "It can make a real difference to partners [as staff are called]. You don't have to be a mutual to share the profit." Sarah Gillard, Director, John Lewis Partnership

105. **Let peers set your bonus:** Carrie Brandes, VP of people at Ubiquity (a California pensions advisory company) explained how they set bonuses. Everybody in the company is given 100 points and can award whatever they see fit to whoever they feel has made an impact to the business or the company. Each person gets a bonus based solely on these peer ratings.

106. **Let peers give awards:** At Google, any employee can give anyone else a $175 cash award, with no management oversight or sign-off required. Laszlo Bock, *Work Rules*.

107. **Receive $200 from the company to thank a colleague:** At Ozvision, each employee can take an extra day off each year,

described as a "day of thanking". They receive $200 in cash from company funds that they can spend however they want to thank a colleague during that day. [Reinventing Organisations, Frederick Laloux]

108. **£5 from your peers:** It doesn't have to be a large sum. "At TNT, all staff were given a supply of £5 M&S vouchers. These could be given to any other person who'd been co-operative and helpful." [Dom Monkhouse, F**K Plan B]

109. **Simple things make a difference:** "We asked staff what was annoying them. The biggest thing was that we had removed tea and coffee. It was five years previously, but still clearly an issue! So we reinstated it and it has made a difference." Polly Neate, CEO, Shelter

110. **Ask your people:** Have you simply asked staff what is bothering them or what would make them happier? Do that, then enable it.

111. **Trust-based HR policies:** "Our people now have unlimited holidays, choose their own working hours and have self-regulated sickness, fully paid. As this approach can lead to people taking fewer vacations, we included a minimum number of days holiday. 'Have fewer rules and trust the team.'" Luke Kyte, Head of Operations, Reddico

112. **Duvet days:** At PossAbilities, staff who have 100% attendance get an extra day off.

113. **Day off on your birthday:** Common in many organisations, including Trinity, Impetus and Adviza. "It is very popular," explains Trinity CEO Steve Hedley.

114. **Liven up Fridays:** "This was an idea from the Happy CEO breakfast. We set a budget of just £15 for people to do something different to liven up Fridays. One group brought in croissants and had a team breakfast, which they are now doing monthly. Another had a sunflower-growing competition. One had a treasure hunt." Katherine Horler, Chief Executive, Adviza

115. **£500 for mental health support:** "We make available £500 to everybody for mental health support. They put it through on expenses, don't even need to go through the line manager. It can be for them or for their family. It has helped a lot with older care and with their kids using it." Simon Biltcliffe, CEO, Webmart

116. **Disability leave:** "We're introducing disability leave [for] disabled colleagues who need to go to appointments for e.g. a new wheelchair, new personal assistants, that wouldn't fit under normal sick leave. Sarah Pugh, CEO, Whizz Kidz

117. **Monthly home-cooked lunch:** "We have a monthly lunch where someone cooks at home and then brings it in to warm up and feed everyone at lunch. A different person cooks each month." Lawrence Parkin, Marketing Manager, Learning Nexus

> "No one should be more than two hundred feet away from food."
> Sergey Brin, Google founder, in *Work Rules*, Laszlo Bock

118. **Fun at work:** Next Jump is a company that believes in enjoying itself, from the summer outing to the annual dance battle. For the latter each office practises relentlessly for the big showdown. Remember that the core job is coding, people not known for their extroversion, and flick through the video[8] of the 2015 event. The new New York office is being built with a swimming pool on the roof, open all weekend with staff encouraged to bring their families.

119. **Play music:** "Play music in toilets!, in reception spaces!, music makes a big difference." Katherine Billingham-Mohammed, Director, Sunshine Group Consulting

Replace appraisals

Is it time to get rid of appraisals, as they don't tend to make people (either employees or managers) happy? Instead replace it with a shorter check-in or snapshot, ideally without a score?

> "Like so many CEOs are discovering, there's no evidence anywhere in the world, in any institution of management science, that existing massive employee evaluation and rating processes are effective."
>
> *It's the Manager*, Jim Clifton, Jim Harper

120. **Get staff to vote on appraisals:** "After a staff vote we got rid of appraisals and replaced them with a one-page snapshot reviewed at a four-monthly check-in." Cathy Busani, Managing Director, Happy

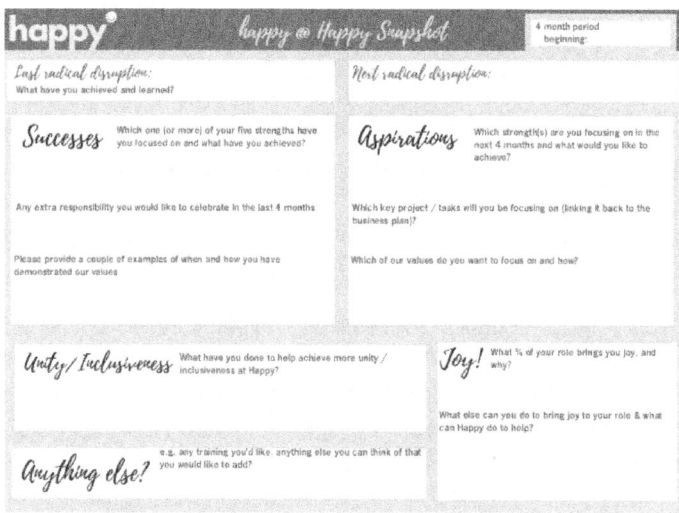

happy *happy @ Happy Snapshot* — 4 month period beginning:

Last radical disruption: What have you achieved and learned?

Next radical disruption:

Successes — Which one (or more) of your five strengths have you focused on and what have you achieved?

Aspirations — Which strength(s) are you focusing on in the next 4 months and what would you like to achieve?

Any extra responsibility you would like to celebrate in the last 4 months

Which key project / tasks will you be focusing on (linking it back to the business plan)?

Please provide a couple of examples of when and how you have demonstrated our values

Which of our values do you want to focus on and how?

Unity / Inclusiveness — What have you done to help achieve more unity / inclusiveness at Happy?

Joy! — What % of your role brings you joy, and why?

What else can you do to bring joy to your role & what can Happy do to help?

Anything else? — e.g. any training you'd like, anything else you can think of that you would like to add?

121. **Appraisals can make performance worse:** Traditional performance appraisals are so bad that they actually make performance worse about one-third of the time. [More Harm Than Good: The Truth About Performance Reviews[9], Robert Sutton, Ben Wigert, Gallup]

122. **$1 billion wasted by appraisals:** One large global professional services company estimated that it was wasting $1 billion of leadership time per year on managers filling out ratings forms rather than developing employees and having ongoing coaching conversations with them. [It's the Manager. Jim Clifton, Jim Harper].

123. **Abolish appraisals:** They don't make people happy and don't serve any useful purpose. "You hear managers saying I'll feed back at their appraisal in two months' time, rather than now when it's needed. Replace appraisals with coaching and one-to-ones. You move from something nobody likes to something they do." Sophie Bryan, Ordinarily Different

> "Who can remember what they've done across a whole year? What's the point of telling someone that they've under-achieved for 12 months?"
> *F**k Plan B*, Dom Monkhouse

124. **Ask about joy:** Ask "what would give you more joy?" instead of "how can we improve your performance?"

125. **Happy and thriving:** "We asked what would lead people to be happy and thriving, which led to some really interesting objectives. If we make it an objective for you to thrive, it brings a much more powerful approach. We have had proper human being conversations," Kate Collins, CEO, Teenage Cancer Trust

126. **Annual feedback from your colleagues:** At tomato processing company Morning Star, people receive feedback at the end of every year from each of the people they have committed to in their CLOU (Colleague Letter of Understanding, where Morning Star staff make commitments to their colleagues).

127. **Try confirmatory practices:** Get your people to think about what they want to achieve or be and then have them score it out of 10 on a regular basis. (Two examples at Happy: "Things are joyful and I'm on top of stuff"; "I was effective and productive today".) With thanks to Helen Sanderson.

128. **But ensure peer-to-peer feedback is sought:** Employees think that co-workers who give them unsolicited advice are self-serving and flaunting their knowledge, but that co-workers who give them solicited advice are being pro-social and want to help them. Unsolicited advice is seen as less useful than solicited advice. (Center for leadership in the future of work[10] 2021)

129. **Abolishing appraisals in a local authority:** In 2018 Hackney Council (in East London) abolished appraisals for all 4,000 staff. They replaced them with regular one-to-ones and quarterly check-ins.

"Our research has suggested that the Check Ins have helped staff members take ownership of their goals and objectives and to think of new ways of achieving them. The most valuable part of the conversation has been the opportunity that they have to talk to their managers about anything (and everything!) that has been happening for them over the past 4-6 weeks in a safe and open space and feel like they are genuinely being listened to." Emily Dathan, who was Senior HR & OD Business Partner at Hackney Council

130. **Peer evaluation over dinner:** At AES, CEO Dennis Bakke installed a practice of team appraisal with his closest peers. They got together once a year, often over dinner in one of their homes to make for a relaxed, informal setting. Every person in turn shared his or her self-evaluation. Other team members commented, questioned or encouraged each other to reach a deeper understanding of their potential and performance.

"Criticism, like rain, should be gentle enough to nourish a man's growth without destroying his roots." Frank Clark, in *Mind Your F**king Business*, Dom Monkhouse.

[Mind Your F**king Business, Dom Monkhouse]

131. **Stop, start, continue at Happy:** We get our people to share what they would like others to stop, start, continue. On my first time, no less than four people said stop leaving the office door open (as we have the café next door, where people talk a lot). It

might seem trivial but it clearly meant a lot to people. And it was something I could very easily do.

They also asked me to listen more...

132. **Buurtzorg: the team members decide how to evaluate each other:** At Buurtzorg, each team holds individual appraisals within the team, based on a competency model that the team has designed. Each team decides what format it will use for these discussions.

"A team I spent time with decided to exchange feedback in subgroups of three colleagues. Everyone prepares a self-evaluation as well as feedback for the other two colleagues in the trio, so people can measure their self-perception against their colleague's perceptions." [Reinventing Organisations, Frederick Laloux]

Recognition

A top-down approach to choosing an "employee of the month" can have mixed results. However if you base it on the views of employees' peers, the results can be different.

133. **Morning praise and thank you:** "ESBZ, the grade 7–12 school in Berlin, has an extraordinary trust and community-building practice based around storytelling: the 'praise meeting'. Every Friday afternoon, the entire school – students, teachers and staff – comes together for an hour in a large hall.

"They always start by singing a song together, to settle into community. All the rest of the time together is unscripted. There is an open microphone on stage, with a simple rule: we are here to praise and thank each other." [Reinventing Organisations, Frederick Laloux]

134. **Share customer delight:** At Zappos they created a WhatsApp group called "Moment of WOW". All staff are members of it and whenever they get great feedback, or do something good for a customer, they share it here. [Leading with Happiness, Alex Kjerulf]

135. **Recognise the assist:** "There is a US basketball team where the manager requires anybody who scores to point at the person who helped them, to recognise the assist. At the start of meetings we used to ask for a win. Now we ask for an assist, something somebody has done to help them." Russell Findlay, CEO, Speakers Trust

136. **Peer recognition:** At Next Jump they have a system of crowd-sourced, peer-nominated rewards to recognise other people's work on a weekly, monthly and annual basis. At one of their annual conferences, in New York, they invited over the parents of the employee receiving the "greatest contribution to others' success" award – all the way from India.

137. **Family get to visit at Haier:** "If someone performs really well, they can invite their family to visit them at their workplace. The country is large, and families often come from far away – their travel is paid for by the company. It's like a short holiday for them, and they can see how their relative is doing. In China, most people consider it a great honour." [Start-Up Factory, Joost Minaar, Pim de Morree, Bran van der Lecq]

Staff first, customers second

The Customer Comes Second (below) was one of the first books I read when I was starting up Happy. It made a big impact on me in terms of helping to create a great place to work.

> Happy employees = Happy customers = Happy results

> "If you want to WOW the customer, first you must WOW the people who WOW the customer."
> *Extreme Humanism*, Tom Peters

138. **Make engagement as important as margins:** "Happy, engaged staff perform better so focus on engagement to get the results you want." Nikki Gatenby, CEO, Propellernet

139. ***Employees First, Customers Second***: That is the title of the book by Vineet Nayar, then CEO of 150,000-strong Indian outsourcing company HCL. He even encouraged his suppliers to adopt the same policy.

140. ***The Customer Comes Second***: This book, by Hal Rosenbluth and Diane Peters, was a key influence on Happy in its early days. Just before publication, Rosenbluth Travel had won the Baldrick award for the best customer service in the entire USA. I often describe the core message as "hire nice people and treat them well".

> "Your employees come first. There's no question about that. If your employees are satisfied and happy and inspired by what they are doing, then they make your customers happy and they come back. We tell our people, 'Don't worry about profit. Think about customer service.' Profit is a by-product of customer service."
> Herb Kelleher, founder of Southwest Airlines

Challenge

When I ask for a time when people have worked at their best, when they are really proud of the results they produced, one feature is being trusted and given freedom. But another is being challenged.

141. **Being thrown in the deep end:** "Within three months of starting at the Department of Health, my manager asked me to address the Public Accounts Committee (equivalent to appearing at a US Senate committee). It was a huge challenge, but he gave me full support, and it was the making of me." This is a quote by a contributor at one of my Happy Workplace sessions.

> "The American psychologist Theodore Isaac Rubin put it like this: Happiness does not come from doing easy work. It comes from the afterglow of satisfaction after the achievement of a difficult task that demands your best."
> *Leading with Happiness*, Alexander Kjerulf

Case Study: Semco

When I read *Maverick* in 1992, it transformed what was then Happy Computers. I went from being a micro-managing boss, who rang every day from holiday to check things were going OK, to – eventually – the head of a fully trust-based environment.

For me *Maverick* is the best business book ever written. I have given copies to many of the staff at Happy and I have also given over 500 copies away to others. For those who don't know, *Maverick* tells the story of Semco, a Brazilian manufacturing company.

Ricardo Semler, the author, explains how he took the company from one where workers were searched every day at the gates (such was the lack of trust) to one where they were fully trusted, set their own targets, chose their managers and – in some cases – even decided their own salary.

It was a truly transformational moment for me and, I know, for many others.

It is still a great read.

142. **Let your people decide:** Semco started by letting people design their uniforms and the colours for the plant. Even that was opposed by existing managers, who reckoned the colours would darken the plant. Semco responded in this way:

"I told [them] our philosophy was to leave such decisions to those who would be living with the consequences."

Following this, Semco then decided to let their workers set their own start and finish times. What if one worker wants to start at 7am and a teammate decides to come in at 9am?

"Our workers knew that production would suffer if they didn't co-ordinate their activities and so that's what they did."

They went on to let the workers decide the layout of the plant. Instead of an assembly line, the workers formed small groups working with different machines.

"The idea was to have, at each of these clusters, a team whose members would fashion a product from beginning to end, giving them accountability for the product's quality and the enormous satisfaction that comes with completing a task."

143. **Set your own targets:** Workers were also given the opportunity to set their own targets. One day a shipment of cutting discs was late, meaning they would miss their targets. Previously the workers would have just stopped working.

Instead, two members of the group visited the supplier, discussed it with the factory workers there and got the discs back on track.

144. **Staff evaluate their managers:** Now, every six months, managers are evaluated by those who work under them. One manager got a mere 40 (out of 100). "After looking into it, we concluded that his subordinates were right: he was a great salesman but a terrible leader. Solution: we made him head of a one-person sales staff and he has shined."

So, Ricardo concluded, "why not let people elect their boss? Seems an utterly sensible way to stop accidents before they are promoted."

145. **Collaborative hiring:** Similarly, "anyone who applies to be a machinist at Semco will be interviewed by a group of machinists, not an executive. They might be able to talk their way past a manager but not people who know everything there is to know about being a machinist."

146. **Get rid of the policies:** And Semler was not keen on policies and procedures: "If you want my advice, take a deep breath, pluck up the courage, and feed the policy manual to the shredder, one page at a time. Let companies be ruled by wisdom from factory to factory and worker to worker."

147. **Good mood or bad mood?:** One of his favourite innovations was the establishment of a board at the plant entrance with the name of each employee and next to it a wooden peg. As each person arrived, he would hang one of three metal tags on the peg: a green tag stood for "Good mood," a yellow tag for "Careful" and a red tag for "Not today – please."

"Forget socialism, capitalism, just-in-time deliveries, salary surveys and the rest of it and concentrate on building organisations that accomplish that most difficult of all challenges: to make people look forward to coming to work in the morning."

148. **Understand the finances:** They also, with the support of their unions, began classes to teach the workers how to read balance sheets, cash-flow statements and other documents – so they understood the finances of Semco.

149. **Could your people do it almost as well?:** If you are a manager, "ask yourself, is it possible that someone else could do this task at least 70% as well as I could. If the answer is Yes, let them."

150. **Take time to think:** "Try blocking out a half day a week on your agenda."

Read Ricardo Semler's book, *Maverick*, or his classic blog, *Managing Without Managers*,[11] written back in 1989.

3. Freedom within Guidelines

I have asked thousands of people whether they prefer "being told what to do", "complete freedom" or "freedom within guidelines". The answers are consistent and vary little between sectors or even between levels of seniority. Very few (under 1% in my experience) want to be told what to do. Some, especially entrepreneurs and CEOs, like complete freedom.

However I find that over 90%, in nearly all environments, want "freedom within guidelines". They want to know the framework they are working within, but then be trusted to use their own judgement. In other words, people want to know what is expected of them, but they want freedom to find the best way to achieve their goals.

> "Freedom + responsibility leads to happiness and performance. That's the equation we used to transform the Belgian Ministry of Social Security."
> Laurence Vanhee, ex-CHO, Belgian Ministry of Social Security

151. **Give full autonomy to make decisions:** At Mayden, Chris May tells me that staff are expected to go through a framework of seven questions and then, if they feel the decision fits them, can make the decision themselves, including spending.

152. **Let your people decide:** "As responsible adults we let our team choose: Where. When. How they work." Laurence Vanhee

153. **Give your staff flexibility in decisions:** "At Timpson the price list is only a guide. Staff can charge what they want." John Timpson

> "Responsible people thrive on freedom and are worthy of freedom. Our model is to increase employee freedom as we grow, rather than limit

it, to continue to attract and nourish innovative people, so we have a better chance of sustained success."

Reed Hastings, in *No Rules Rules*, Reed Hastings, Erin Meyer

154. **Set up your own Leadership Team:** At the Mexican software company Nearsoft staff can set up a Leadership Team in response to a perceived issue. One example was year-end bonuses, which some felt weren't fair. The Leadership Team – set up by members of staff – proposed changes, tested it out and, after refinement, implemented the new approach across the organisation. [Worldblu, 50 Transformation Practices].

Get people to set their own targets

If your people are motivated and feel in control, they are likely to set tougher targets than managers, feel better about them and be more likely to achieve them.

155. **The one-minute target at GCHQ**: GCHQ is the government's intelligence and security organisation. The Head of IT described how, after reading *The Happy Manifesto*, he let his people set their targets.

He gave the example of their tech support people. With security concerns at the forefront, it used to take two weeks to check out a laptop. "It was clear we needed to shorten it. If it had been left to me to set the target, then I would have probably set it at one day – a huge improvement on where we were. We left it to the team. They set the target at five minutes. When they achieved that, they reduced it to two minutes. They have now got it down to one minute." (Spark the Change Conference, 2016).

156. **Use direct feedback to help people set targets:** At Happy I sat down with Natalie, who had just taken over credit control, to agree targets. At the time we were owed £135,000. Instead of setting a target, I asked Natalie to send me a spreadsheet every fortnight, showing how much we were owed in total, at 30 days and at 90 days – key information I needed.

I then asked her to set her targets for the next report. The first time she set a very low figure and didn't make it. The second, she was conservative and overachieved it. As time went on, she became clearer and also very focused on achieving the target she had set. Within 12 months the amount owed had dropped to £35,000, less than it had been in years.

157. **At Geonetric, staff "map their choices":** Quarterly, each team reviews Geonetric's overall priorities, and creates a team Impact Map of how they will contribute. In turn each individual creates their own Impact Map. They choose, for each of the

team's goals, whether they want to lead the initiative, provide support or provide advice during the process – and to what level? [Worldblu, 50 Transformational Practices.]

158. **Let teenagers set their own curfew time:** Michelle Obama describes how her parents used guidelines rather than rules. As teenagers they never had a fixed curfew. "Instead they'd ask 'What's a reasonable time for you to be home?' and then trust us to stick to our word." [Becoming, Michelle Obama]

> "If you set a crazy, ambitious goal and miss it, you'll still achieve something remarkable."
> Larry Page, Google founder, in *Work Rules*, Laszlo Bock

Or have no targets at all

> "People with targets and jobs dependent upon meeting them will probably meet the targets, even if they have to destroy the enterprise to do it."
> W. Edwards Deming

159. **No targets, no goals?** That is the approach at the successful software company Basecamp. "You can absolutely run a great business without a single goal. You don't need something fake to do something real. And if you must have a goal, how about just staying in business? Or serving your customers well? Or being a delightful place to work? Just because these goals are harder to quantify does not make them any less important. We don't do grand plans at Basecamp – not for the company, not for the product. There's no five-year plan. No three-year plan. No one-year plan. Nada.

"Every six weeks or so, we decide what we'll be working on next. And that's the only plan we have. Anything further out is considered a 'maybe, we'll see'. The sooner you admit you have no idea what the world will look like in five years, three years, or even one year, the sooner you'll be able to move forward without the fear of making the wrong big decision years in advance."[It doesn't have to be crazy at work, Jason Fried and David Heinemeier Hansson]

> "A company's job isn't to empower people; it is to remind people that they walk in the door with power and to create the conditions for them to exercise it. Do that, and you will be astonished by the great work they will do for you."
> *Powerful*, Patty McCord

Systems not rules

Rules require you to do something even if it does not make sense. Systems enable you to try something different if it does make sense.

160. **Guidelines not rules:** At the Hyatt Hotel there used to be 24 rules that staff would have to follow when checking in a guest. When they changed it to "treat our clients as you would a guest in your own home", customer satisfaction rose by 80%. [Happy as a Dane, Malene Rydahl].

161. **Forget the manuals and policies:** "Get your people to be more human at work and just do the right thing." Donna Reeves, ex-Director, Kingfisher plc

162. **Regularly attack the problem:** At Google there is an annual programme called Bureaucracy Busters where Googlers identify their biggest frustrations and help fix them. [Work Rules, Laszlo Bock]

163. **Just one rule at Nordstrom:** US department store Nordstrom, famous for its customer service, issues new employees with a card stating the one rule: "Use good judgement in all situations. Please feel free to ask your department manager, store manager, or human resources officer any question at any time." [Team of Teams, Stanley McChrystal]

164. **'Make a Friend' instead of processes and call handling times:** At United Utilities they moved from call scripts and measurement of call handling times. "Instead", explained Customer Services Director Louise Beardmore, "I said to people, you are all adults and I want you to talk to customers like they are friends.

"The step change that we have seen in performance is immense. I am averaging about 140 to 160 thank yous or WOW awards from customers who have spontaneously given me feedback about employees."

Innovation

How can you ensure a culture of innovation?

> "If you know where you're heading, you're not innovating. If things work out as planned, you weren't chasing anything interesting."
> *The Excellence Dividend*, Tom Peters

165. **At GCHQ there is one day a month set aside for innovation:** On this day they use a dedicated collaborative space to promote new thinking. Posters are presented, workshops are run and experts from the community come to talk about their fields. Each day has a theme with a challenge designed to inspire new collaborations throughout the day.

The introduction of innovation days took the proportion of staff actively engaged in innovative projects from 18% of the workforce to 82%. A key target of the days is finding more efficient ways to do previously manual tasks. For one highly disruptive project (changing how fundamental processes are followed at the core of GCHQ) it resulted in halving costs and a 32% reduction in time to completion. More here.[12]

166. **Ask your customers:** The Arsenal food store is a convenience shop close to the football club's Emirates Stadium in North London. It won a local customer service award based on one simple method. The owner asks people who come into the shop what they would like that isn't stocked there already – and orders it.

A simple and obvious step. But have you ever been asked in any shop what you would like them to stock? How often do you ask that question of your customers?

> "In a company born to innovate, the risk is not innovating. The real risk is to think it is safe to play safe."
> Jony Ive, ex-Chief Design Officer, Apple

Feedback

Should managers give feedback or should peers? Or should you set things up so it is clear from the metrics how well you are doing?

> "Almost half (47%) of employees report that they received feedback from their manager 'a few times or less' in the past year. What's more, only 26% of employees strongly agree that the feedback they receive helps them do their work better."
>
> *It's the Manager*, Jim Clifton, Jim Harper

167. **Use peer feedback:** "Research has shown peers have twice as much impact as anything your manager does." Alison Sturgess-Durden, Director, Mayden

168. **Let people own the metrics:** A key metric for a training business is trainer utilisation (how much of the cost of a course goes on the trainer), though trainers are more likely to be focused on the equally important measure of customer feedback. As we moved to embed the Happy culture, trainers were asked to take full responsibility and complete a simple spreadsheet each month to report back on their utilisation.

It produced a new focus for them and for support staff, giving them the key information they needed. As a result the proportion of course income that went on the trainer fell from 42% to 29% (more than doubling the level of profit across the business).

169. **Decide when you want feedback:** At Indian outsourcing company HCL, employees can ask for feedback using the EPIC (Employee Passion Indicative Count) survey. This evaluates employee passion, motivating factors and personal strengths. But it is up to the individual to decide whether they want the feedback and when to make it happen. [Worldblu, 50 transformational practices]

170. **Choose your questions and who you want to hear from:** This is a neat idea from Aaron Dignan. Ask each member of your team whether they'd like feedback at all, whether they'd like to use standard questions (such as stop/start/continue) or would rather choose their own, and who they would like to receive feedback from.

"Send the questions to their suggested colleagues with a time limit for contribution. Make this a ritual that is prioritised and celebrated in the culture. Compile and share the responses with each participant. Let them choose who to share it with, including their manager (if they have one)." [Brave New Work, Aaron Dignan]

171. **Being clear on what is wrong:** Apple's Chief Design Officer Jony Ive told a story about a time when he pulled his punches when criticising his team's work. When Steve Jobs asked Jony why he hadn't been clearer about what was wrong, Jony replied, "Because I care about the team." To which Steve replied, "No, Jony, you're just really vain. You just want people to like you." Recounting the story, Jony said, "I was terribly cross because I knew he was right." [Radical Candour, Kim Scott]

172. **Beyond 360-degree evaluation:** Most big companies now get managers to be evaluated by peers and by some of those they manage. HCL's innovation was to open this up, so you could evaluate anybody in the company that you came into contact with. As well as the widespread feedback, the unexpected result was that managers began to be judged by how many responses they received. It became a measure of their circle of influence. [Employees First, Customers Second, Vineet Nayar]

Case Study: Reddico

A journey into a self-managing organisation

Reddico is a software development and digital marketing company, employing a few dozen people on a farm near Tonbridge in Kent.

Head of Operations Luke Kyte explains the philosophy here: "No hours. No managers. Rules set by the team. Let's see what happens next."

Inspired by *The Happy Manifesto*, Reddico started the move to becoming self-managing in March 2018. Just 18 months later it resulted in happier employees, more satisfied customers, higher revenue and a big increase in profits.

173. **No managers, just coaches:** They have moved away from having line managers and instead provide their people with coaches. "To be a coach we insisted you went on the Level 5 leadership programme at Happy", explains Head of Operations Luke Kyte.

The Level 5 programme is based on an Apprenticeship Standard, so 95% of the cost is paid by the UK government, meaning it only costs £350 per person for almost two years of personal development.

"It's great," continues Luke. "It's really interesting how much you can learn, new skills, new ways of communicating. I have really enjoyed self-awareness and increasing awareness of others – understanding how different people can react to different circumstances. It has made a real difference."

Making the change

174. **It is not about free food:** "Back in 2017 we thought we had got the culture right. We had free food, a beer fridge, a table tennis table, Xbox, all the things we thought you needed for a happy workplace."

"We did the Employee Net Promoter Score (NPS) and thought we would get 'World Class'. In fact we got just Good, with some people scoring as passives or detractors. At first I took it quite personally. We were giving all this for free, it seemed ungrateful. Then you start to look at it and think it must be us, must be something going on internally.

"We realised it's not how much you give people for free but how you can free people to give more.

"We looked around and started to get inspiration from books like *The Happy Manifesto* and *Maverick*. We talked to the team, to get insight of what they wanted."

175. **Focus on the output:** "Now we focus on how people can do what they need to get the job done. Instead of having people work 9–5, controlling the input, we focus on the output. It has been a massive change. Some people work best in morning, some in afternoon, some in evening, why do we pigeonhole people?

"Before it was a bit erratic. One person might ask their line manager if they could work from home and get it. Another might not and ask why not? There was confusion and frustration."

176. **Trust people:** "We started with our own manifesto, 6,000 words long. As in *The Happy Manifesto*, it came round to values of trust, believing the best in people, giving people that power to do the job in the way they wanted to.

"Then we put the red flags in place: targets (which staff set themselves), NPS, quarterly 360 review – so if something went wrong, we would know about it. To be honest, I looked at it and didn't know if it would work. How can we give all this freedom, surely something will go wrong?"

As much holiday as you want

177.   **Unlimited holiday, but with a minimum:** "They now all work whatever pattern they like and take as much holiday as they want. Though we have set a minimum of 20 days."

Do people actually take lots of holiday? "Well I've taken 30 days already this year and it is only August."

178.   **No managers:** "Not having managers was the bit I was most confused about. Who is responsible for reviews, salary setting, I wondered. But we moved from managers to having two separate roles: department leads are responsible for growing the department and setting strategy. Coaches support and empower people and everybody picks their own coach. Salaries are now decided by a panel elected by the staff."

2018 had been a great year for the company for revenue. However in 2019 Reddico, after adopting this approach, has increased revenue and profit every month. "And not just by a small amount. In May it was something like a 130% increase in profit."

World class ENPS

179.   **The Employee NPS is now 95:** This is a phenomenal figure. I know of only one other company at that level. The client NPS – measuring client satisfaction – has also gone up, from around 60 to 80, which is "World Class".

180.   **Freedom and trust:** "What's the secret? We don't have a hard set of rules in place. We just give freedom and trust and responsibility. We say 'This is how we do it, go ahead and show us you can. Just don't have a negative impact on the team with what you are doing.'

"*The Happy Manifesto* was a massive part of it. All the principles behind *The Happy Manifesto*, we drew as inspiration for our own manifesto. The beliefs, that shift from being a traditional hierarchical business to giving more trust for the team."

181. **Democratic salaries:** The Reddico salary approach is similar to Happy's. A salary panel of four is elected by the staff and they decide what rise employees should get.

182. **Go for it:** What tips does Luke have for others embarking on the journey to a trust-based workplace? "Believe in it. Go for it. Take it in small manageable steps. Have a plan for what you are trying to do. Break it down into what will make the biggest impact first.

"It took us nine months to fully roll it out. I had to be freed up to do it. I needed to be solely responsible. You have to have someone dedicated to doing it. Otherwise it gets talked about and promised, but will not happen."

Has anything gone wrong in the transition? "No, not that I can think of."

Could you create a self-managing organisation? Are you ready to give your people the trust and freedom to do a great job?

4. Be Open and Transparent

> "Without information you cannot take responsibility. With information you cannot avoid responsibility."
>
> Jan Carlzon, CEO, SAS Airlines (1981–94)

That Carlzon quote is one of my favourites. At Happy all information – finances, salaries etc. – is available to all staff. How else do you ensure full responsibility and accountability? The only exception would be anything about an individual that they would want to keep confidential.

183. **Share everything:** When Darren Childs became CEO of UKTV, he reduced the barriers between leaders and employees by sharing information about the company's finances and the performance reviews of the leadership team. He also allowed all employees to ask him anything they wanted at their weekly Town Hall staff meetings, with all questions added to a box that was opened on stage at the meeting.

184. **Share the financial information:** "At W. L. Gore we've got a core value which is belief in the individual and we believe that everybody walking into work wants to do a good job. We place trust immediately you walk in the door. So if someone comes into the door and they want to know what the financial situation is, as a leader I'll say: 'Yeah, this is it, this is where we're at.'

"We're very open with information, we trust people. Because if you haven't got the information, how can you make decisions?" (John Housego at the 2016 Happy Workplaces conference)

185. **Share and people take responsibility:** In 2012 I was away from the office and somebody asked our Finance Manager what the bank balance was. She knows we share all information so she told them. Then they asked how much it was a month before and three months before. As they delved more deeply it was clear there was a serious problem.

By the time I got back in the office, just a few days later, they had formed an action group to deal with it and had already identified tens of thousands of pounds of potential savings. That taking of responsibility was a key moment in turning Happy round.

186.　**Total finance transparency:** At Happy we make all finance records available to our staff, and explain to them how to use them. However, we are a private company. Netflix does this as a public company. If anybody uses information to buy shares, knowing they are set to go up, it can be a criminal offence.

Indeed before they show the figures, they show this slide: "You go to jail if you trade on this … Or if your friend does. Confidential. Do not share."

187.　**Total transparency:** Err on the side of sharing more information than people need. At Happy we make all information available for everybody to see (apart from any personal and disciplinary stuff).

188.　**Move competence down to the front line:** "Take Morning Star, the world's largest tomato processor. It has no managers and all key investment decisions are taken by individuals who in other organisations would be regarded as 'blue collar' employees. Most of these employees are capable of sophisticated financial modelling – they can calculate the net present value and internal rate of return of new investments.

"Instead of moving decisions upward at Morning Star, they have moved competence down – to individuals who have the information and the context to make the best decisions." [Age of Agile, Stephen Denning]

189.　**Make all manager plans public:** Previously at HCL the 300 most senior managers had prepared their plans for the next level up. Instead the company published them all to all staff in the MyBlueprint portal, so they could see and compare them. As well as increasing transparency, CEO Vineet Nayar comments that it led to much more work being put into getting the plans right.

190. **Share your CEO Problems:** At HCL Vineet Nayar decided to create a portal to share the problems he was having difficulty solving as CEO and the challenges he saw for the company. He involved the whole company in understanding his role, the big picture and in coming up with solutions. (from Employees first, Customers Second, Vineet Nayar)

> Our standing guidance was "Share information until you're afraid it's illegal."
> *Team of Teams*, Stanley McChrystal

191. **If the data is clear and public, people want to improve:** At Dutch care company Buurtzorg, where the nurses are organised into teams of ten to twelve, the productivity of each team is listed regularly in a table. "Teams at the bottom are motivated to improve out of pride; they don't need a boss to discuss how they could improve," explains Frederick Laloux. [Reinventing Organisations, Frederick Laloux]

192. **Full transparency at HCL:** The Indian conglomerate HCL introduced full transparency of the performance of every unit in the company. Seeing their benchmarks, and being able to compare their performance with others, increased shared learning and provided powerful incentives to improve.

193. **At Nucor employees are responsible for maximising margins:** "Nucor, the most consistently profitable steel company in the world, practises radical transparency. Every single associate knows the profitability of every order that ships. At Nucor, it is the frontline employees, not managers, who are responsible for maximizing margins." [The Age of Agile, Stephen Denning]

194. **At Haier all information is available to all employees:** "At each workplace, screens display all relevant information for employees. How many products have they made? How many have been sold? How many orders are there? How close are they to the daily target? How much money have they earned? All this and more can be established at the touch of a button." This can turn all employees into financial experts. [Start-Up Factory, Joost Minaar, Pim de Morree, Bran van der Lecq]

195. **No triangulation:** "We agreed that if one person complained to another or had concerns about that person, then the complainer had 72 hours to hold a conversation directly with that individual.

"One time, a global leader (we'll call him Bob) shared with me some problems he was having with a sales director (we'll call her Olivia). I told Bob he had 72 hours to talk to Olivia. He didn't, and I kept my end of the bargain and had a conversation with Olivia about the concerns. Bob said, "I can't believe you told her what I told you." I replied, "I told you that's how we behave in this organisation." Bob soon left the organisation. [Mind Your F**king Business, Dom Monkhouse]

196. **Financial literacy at New Belgium Brewing:** After workers answered 50%, when asked what percentage of income went to profit, the company introduced open-book finances. Now there are finance classes – including how to read profit-and-loss reports. Finances are reported at each monthly meeting. {Worldblu, 50 transformational practices)

> "Assume that all information can be shared with the team, instead of assuming that no information can be shared. Restricting information should be a conscious effort, and you'd better have a good reason for doing so. In open source, it's countercultural to hide information."
>
> *Work Rules*, Laszlo Bock.

Communication

How good is your communication?

197. **Floor to Board in five minutes:** Liz Mouland is Chief Nurse at First Community, and recalls: "We wanted to design something that was not non-hierarchical but was an inverted hierarchy. We see the function of the Board and of management is to support those providing excellent care and services to the public.

"One example of how we do this is our 'Floor to Board in five minutes'. Any of our 450 staff can contact a Board member within five minutes. Out of hours they can use the 24/7 On Call Manager phone number who can escalate to a Board member if appropriate."

198. **Remove the door from your office**: Another example is the organisation's open-door policy. Liz, as clinical lead for the organisation, literally has no door on her office. "We have a behaviours framework which we expect everybody to role model. It is about showing emotional intelligence, with warmness and friendliness, where everybody's voice matters."

199. **Remove the wall from your office:** The new CEO at UKTV wanted to reduce the barriers between leaders and staff, so one of his first acts was to take the walls off his office.

200. **Brutal honesty at Mindvalley:** Each week at this Malaysian education company, CEO Vishan Lacklani conducts a "brutal honesty" session. Employees can anonymously ask any question they want and the founders must answer them openly and authentically. It is said to create a climate of healthy dialogue, deep listening and trust. [Worldblu, 50 transformational practices]

201. **Tell Me, direct link to Director at United Utilities**: "I introduced this thing called Tell Me. You can tell me anything you want to tell me, any day. You can tell me if you are fed up. You can tell me if I am doing something stupid. There is not a form; there is not a process. I have an email address for Tell Me. They come

through every day – between 40 and 45 every single day. They are everything from 'Louise, why does it say this on the bill because that telephone number isn't right'. Or 'Louise, I spoke to a customer today and actually I think it would be better if this tariff were designed in this way'. Or 'Louise, I am hacked off because I have just been given my holiday allocation and I don't like it'.

"So what is your mechanism for hearing your employee voice and how complicated have you made it? Because if it is complicated or it's a case of 'I tried to tell you once but nobody did anything', then I am not going to bother again." Louise Beardmore, Customer Services Director, United Utilities, at the 2017 Happy Workplaces Conference.

202. **Try two-minute Tuesday:** "Every Tuesday I record a two-minute video on what's going on, and distribute it to all our people. The good stuff and the difficult stuff." Derek Hill, MD, ATS

203. **What colour are your balls?:** At Dreamhost, a container at the exit contains red, yellow and green balls. Every member of staff places a ball when they leave the office (green for great day, red for bad, yellow for in the middle). The number of balls of each colour is recorded each day at each location. Those leaving red are encouraged to leave a note of explanation, which the leadership reads daily. [Worldblu, 50 transformational practices]

204. **Everyone must have the freedom to communicate with anyone:** At Pixar members of any department can approach anyone in another department to solve problems without having to go through "proper" channels.

It also means that managers need to learn that they don't always have to be the first to know about something going on in their realm, and it's OK to walk into a meeting and be surprised. The impulse to tightly control the process is understandable given the complex nature of movie-making, but problems are almost by definition unforeseen. The most efficient way to deal with numerous problems is to trust people to work out the difficulties directly with each other without having to check for permission. Click here.[13]

205. **Enable chance encounters, again at Pixar:** "Our building, which is Steve Jobs's brainchild, is another way we try to get people from different departments to interact. Most buildings are designed for some functional purpose, but ours is structured to maximize inadvertent encounters.

"At its center is a large atrium, which contains the cafeteria, meeting rooms, bathrooms, and mailboxes. As a result, everyone has strong reasons to go there repeatedly during the course of the workday. It's hard to describe just how valuable the resulting chance encounters are."

Open salaries

If you have full transparency of your finances, should salaries also be transparent?

206. **Publicly available salaries at Buffer:** At the online software company, not only are salaries available internally, but they publish them on their website for all to see. Within the first month of posting this, Buffer doubled the number of job applicants they received.[14]

207. **It's about fairness:** At Glitch (previously called Fog Creek Software) all salaries are shared internally. "Transparency isn't the goal," explains Anil Dash, Glitch's CEO. "The goal is paying everyone fairly, and transparency forces us to do that." More information here.[15]

208. **See every salary people have ever earned:** At Happy we have a spreadsheet, which is available to anybody internally, which details both current salary and every salary people have ever earned at the company – together with the reasons for each increase. Give people full information and they are more likely to make good decisions.

209. **Internally available salaries:** Companies at which staff can see everybody's salary include Piscina International, Whole Foods, Namaste Solar, CareerFoundry, Crowdfunder, SumAll and many more.

Case Study: Belgian Federal Office of Social Affairs

> "How people feel and think determines their behaviour. So focus on making them feel good."
> Laurence Vannhee, ex-CHO

When Frank van Massenhove took over the Belgian Federal Officer of Social Affairs in 2002, he was determined to create freedom and responsibility for the employees.

210. **Results not hours:** One of his first steps was to allow employees to work when they want and where they want. Even before the pandemic there were typically only 150 people present in the office, out of a workforce of 1,070.

People are evaluated solely on the results, not on the number of working hours. Frank estimates that people work an average 30 hours a week, as does he.

211. **Happy employees:** Frank posed this question to the workforce: "How do we build a government department aimed at customer satisfaction and results-driven work, where the employees are happy?

"The goal was to make civil servants happy and create a more efficient government," Frank explains in *Making Work Fun*, the book by Corporate Rebels.

The book describes how "productivity rose by 18% during the first three years, and after that by an average of 10% per year. The ministry has the lowest number of illness-related absences in Belgium, and there is virtually no burnout."

212. **Burn the box:** "Don't just think outside the box, burn the box," explains Laurence. "When we brought in flexible working the receptionists asked if they could work from home. We assumed that wouldn't work. But they teamed up with some of the admin

staff, agreed a shared workload and got to work at home some days of the week. Think differently.

"It is about trust: move from command and control to trust of your people. Your leaders should be facilitators, not experts."

213. **Collective objectives:** Also, use collective objectives: "Individual objectives are bullsh*t. We got people to set collective objectives to work towards together, and productivity increased by 20%.

Freedom + responsibility lead to happiness and performance: "That's the equation we used to transform the Belgian Ministry of Social Security."

214. **Kisssify the process:** "Keep it sexy, keep it simple, keep it sustainable. If the process or policies don't fit that, get them changed."

Initially Frank changed from five levels of hierarchy to two. Now a major section of the department has become self-managing.

215. **Show people's talents:** Saskia Gheysens explains in a Corporate Rebels article: "We see that in the new structure people stand up and display talents we haven't seen before. They have more opportunity now to show their talent – they have really started to flourish."

Don't tell the politicians!

How did politicians react to these changes? Frank didn't tell them! "I kept my mouth shut until we achieved the necessary results."

However the proportion of civil service applicants wanting to work for the department has gone from 18% in 2002 to 93% now. And they now have 57 applicants, on average, for each vacancy – compared to 3 before the transformation.

5. Recruit for Attitude, Train for Skill

Instead of qualifications and experience, recruit on attitude and potential ability. Use collaborative hiring and get people, as much as possible, to do the job in the interview.

Recruit for attitude

216. **Hire for humility at Next Jump:** Many companies now say they "hire for attitude, train for skill". At Next Jump they hire for one specific attitude. "We used to screen for skills. And we ended up with a lot of brilliant jerks," explains joint UK Managing Director Tarun Gidoomal. "So now we hire for humility."

In the two talks I've seen Next Jump executives give, that has been very evident. What has stood out has been both the humility and vulnerability they were prepared to show.

217. **Recruit for personality at Timpson:** "We can teach them how to cut keys and repair shoes," explained Timpson founder John Timpson.

218. **When Google learnt skills weren't enough:** In a period of extreme growth, 2005–8, there was a focus on hiring people with the right skills. In 2007 they realised they were having challenges in some of the people they'd recruited, which were picked up especially in the regular Googlegeist, the employee satisfaction survey. Google realised they had veered off in their hiring practice and had brought in senior people with a more command-and-control approach, "which doesn't work at Google at all". The response was to dramatically improve the hiring process, to help people understand their culture and weed out people who have a "tell" approach. Yvonne Agnei, at the 2013 Happy Workplaces Conference.

219. **Get the team to write the job description and set the salary:** "Instead of the manager writing the job spec and setting the salary, we got the team to do it. They will be working with them and, as our salaries are transparent, they know what everybody else is earning and are best placed to decide the right amount for the new recruit." Cathy Busani, Happy

220. **Make them fall in love with you!:** Finally, always be clear that the recruitment process should be as much about giving them a positive picture of your company (whether or not they get the job) as solely meeting your needs. As Laszlo Bock puts it: "Remember too that you don't just want to assess the candidate. You want them to fall in love with you. Really. You want them to have a great experience, have their concerns addressed, and come away feeling like they just had the best day of their lives." [Work Rules, Laszlo Bock]

221. **Google looks for people who are "Googly":** "We look for a cultural fit with the company," explained Yvonne Agnei – then Google Head of Benefits – at the 2013 Happy Workplaces Conference. This includes a passion for what you do, and interests beyond work. "We like people who travel, we like people who speak more than one language and engage with their community. Now we don't hire people if we don't think they are 'googly'. If they mis-treated the receptionist or came across as arrogant, we would not hire them whatever their skills."

222. **Or does it?:** "Truth be told, some of our most effective colleagues are people we most definitely would not want to have a beer with. (In a few rare instances they are people we would rather pour a beer on.)" [How Google works, Eric Schmidt]

223. **Hire from a different industry:** Dom Monkhouse explains that at Rackspace, an IT server company, they didn't hire customer service people from the IT industry. "They came from retail and hospitality. That's because you can't be successful at serving in a bar or restaurant and hate human beings." [Mind Your F**king Business, Dom Monkhouse]

224. **Forward or backward looking:** Backward-looking recruitment focuses on CVs and qualifications. Forward-focused recruitment looks at potential. "We changed the job description to need to be, need to do, need to know," says Sarah Pugh, CEO, Whizz Kidz.

Get people to do the job in the interview

Most interviews are based on questions. Candidates are asked how they performed well in a team or solved a problem, or whatever is needed for the job. The danger is that you will recruit somebody who is good at talking about how they would do the job, rather than good at doing the job. An alternative is to get people to perform the key tasks that are involved in the job.

225. **Get them to do a real project in the interview:** "At Basecamp we put a real project in front of the candidates so that they can show us what they can do. For example, when we're choosing a new designer, we hire each of the finalists for a week, pay them $1,500 for that time, and ask them to do a sample project for us. Then we have something to evaluate that's current, real, and completely theirs.

"It's the same kind of work they'd be doing if they got the job." [It doesn't have to be crazy at work, Jason Fried and David Heinemeier Hansson]

226. **The best predictor is to get people to do a sample of work:** Laszlo Bock refers to the work by Frank Schmidt and John Hunter, who in 1998 published a meta-analysis of 85 years of research on how well assessments predict performance. None of the methods fully predict but the single best predictor of how someone will perform in a job is a work sample test, at 29%.

"We do our interviewing based on really testing your skills. Like, write some code, explain this thing, right? Not look at your résumé, but really see what you can do." [Work Rules, Laszlo Bock]

227. **Doing the job as a headteacher:** As Chair of Governors of Stoke Newington School, I ensured that when we recruited a new headteacher, they performed some of the key roles. They had to meet with students and parents. They held a management meeting with the two most difficult departments. And they ran a

full staff meeting. And, in all those cases, we got all those involved to feed back.

We also had three formal interviews, as required by the local authority. The candidate who would have succeeded in those formal interviews was very different from the one who succeeded in the activities.

Collaborative hiring

If only one or two people are involved in the recruitment, the danger is that they will recruit somebody like them.

228. **Apple: involve people from other parts of the business:** At Apple you can easily interact with a dozen people in the recruitment process, any of which can be decisive. As Steve Jobs explained, "When we hire someone, even if they are going to be in marketing, I will have them talk to the design folks and the engineers."

229. **Pret A Manger: the team decides whether to take them on:** Once somebody has passed the initial screening at UK coffee and sandwich chain Pret A Manger, they work a day in one of the branches. At the end of the day all the staff in that branch take a vote on whether to take them on permanently. The aim is to find people who are "friendly and lively ... people who are good-humoured by nature." And anybody who has been to Pret (I have a colleague who never goes anywhere else) will testify that they definitely succeed in finding those people.

230. **Make your partner look good:** In what *Inc.* magazine described as "[The Most Unusual – and Effective – Hiring Process You'll Ever See](#)", Menlo Innovations founder Richard Sheridan explains how they threw out the résumés, questions and fancy ads and instead hold mass auditions for people who will fit the culture.

Menlo is a coding company and, unusually, the programmers work in pairs (with just one computer). So the interviewees get to work in pairs, switching every 20 minutes and observed by Menlo staff. The team, not the managers, make the hiring decisions. And you get through if you show authentic collaboration, confidence and humility. As Sheridan puts it: "We explain to the candidates their goal is to make their pair partners look good enough to be invited back for the next stage of evaluation."

231. **Involve the team and the clients:** "For careers advisers and support workers we get the shortlist and they go out and meet the teams. We always involve young people, our clients, too. Our people get the final say in who they will work with." Katherine Horler, Chief Executive, Adviza

232. **Google: "Don't leave the interviewing to the bosses!":** That is the advice of Laszlo Bock, Head of People at Google. He explains that you may meet your future boss at an interview, but far more important is to meet and be judged by those who will work for you, and also people with no connection to the job. "This sends a strong signal to candidates about Google being non-hierarchical, and it also helps prevent cronyism, where managers hire their old buddies for their new teams." [Work Rules, Laszlo Bock]

233. **Facebook: check the team dynamic:** Julie Zhou, Director of Product Design, explains how Facebook likes to get a candidate to work with several other designers to evaluate the team dynamic. They look over one another's work, provide feedback and get to see what they are like to work with in practice.

234. **$3,000 to leave at Zappos:** The US online shoe retailer Zappos is famous for its stunning customer service and for its policy of offering new hires $3,000 to leave at the end of their training. The idea is they only want people who want to work at Zappos enough to forego that offer. As well as those that interview them, candidates will go through a "social test" of attending some type of department meeting and getting others to interact informally with them.

Zappos also likes to send a car to pick up the candidate. Founder Tony Hsieh explains: "It doesn't matter how well the day of interviews went, if our shuttle driver wasn't treated well, then we won't hire that person."

235. **Semco hires by democratic vote:** Brazilian company Semco was the original inspiration for the ideas of trust and freedom that we espouse at Happy. The company moved from one where it was

led from the top to one where autonomous work teams had control over their job. This includes setting their own targets and production goals and also to hiring (and firing) both staff and supervisors by democratic vote.[16]

236. **Southbank Centre makes it fun, interactive and relevant:** At the Southbank Centre in London (the UK's largest arts centre), they used to recruit "hosts" using a traditional application form and interview. But then they realised that the hosts, who are the people who guide you around and show you to your seat, never have to write anything. A process focused on how good their written answers were did not make sense.

So they decided to invite applicants in 200 at a time. The candidates get to find out about the South Bank, interact with each other and meet a whole range of staff. Those who are best with people get invited back, based on a wide range of staff views. They feel it's been much more effective. One interesting by-product is that the people who get employed tend to be older than before.

237. **Happy interviews in groups:** I like to think we practise what we preach at Happy and seek to involve lots of people in the interview. We always interview candidates in groups, to see how people work together and get involved with those who will work with them. For recruitment as a customer service person, every existing person in customer service will get to sit in and have a say in who is chosen.

238. **Try the pizza test:** "We added an extra stage to recruitment where the new person meets their colleagues-to-be, maybe for pizza or another meal, to ensure the right fit. So far all have been accepted and it's really increased buy-in." Luke Kyte, Reddico

239. **Ask the team:** "We needed a new HR manager, so we asked the HR team to go out and recruit and find two candidates they were happy with. They did all the pre-interviewing, leaving me and my deputy to meet those final two. Rather than a formal interview, we just shared with them two difficult HR cases. The

person we hired is a great fit for the organisation and compliments the other members of the team fantastically." Katherine Horler, Chief Executive, Adviza

240. **Don't ask for qualifications:** For a doctor it probably does make sense to have a medical degree. However for most professions, does a qualification make sense? If you are asking for generic degrees, for instance, maybe it is because you want to hire somebody like yourself.

241. **It doesn't matter how smart you are:** "We don't pay too much attention to résumés. We are more interested in culture fit. We don't start with how smart you are. We don't care what you've learned. We aren't interested in where you've gone to college. None of that matters if you don't fit our culture. Once we've determined that there is a fit with our culture, then we start to ask about skills." Richard Sheridan, Menlo Innovations, in *Age of Agile*, Stephen Denning.

242. **When Google required a degree and lost some of the most talented people in Silicon Valley:** There was a crazy-strict rule in Google's Product Management that you had to have a computer science degree to join the team. Many people wanted to transfer to Product because they had ideas they wanted to pursue, but they were prevented because they didn't have the right degree.

One was Biz Stone who, stymied by the rule, left Google to co-found Twitter. Another was Ben Silbermann who, similarly blocked, left Google to found Pinterest. Kevin Systrom also left Google to co-found Instagram when he couldn't join the PM team because of his college degree. [Radical Candour, Kim Scott]

(Google ex-CEO Eric Schmidt confirms this story in *How Google Works*. He describes how Salar Kamangar wanted to get Kevin onto the APM (Associate Product Manager) programme. He argued that the young associate was a self-taught programmer and had a "history of working closely with engineers and shipping things". However, others stuck to the degree rule and denied the transfer, causing Kevin to leave and found Instagram.

243. **Ignore their education at Basecamp:** "On top of not considering provenance or location, we don't consider formal education, either. We look at people's actual work, not at their

diploma or degree. [It doesn't have to be crazy at work, Jason Fried and David Heinemeier Hansson]

244. **Google used to ask for degrees, until they did the research:** Laszlo Bock, Google Head of People, describes how in 2010 their "analyses revealed that academic performance didn't predict job performance beyond the first two or three years after college, so we stopped requiring grades and transcripts except from recent graduates.

"We now prefer to take a bright, hardworking student who graduated from the top of her class at a state school over an average or even above-average Ivy League grad," he says, adding "Some of our best performers never set foot on a college campus." [Work Rules, Laszlo Bock]

245. **Teach your people the required skills between the interview and starting work:** In the airline industry it is normal for swimming ability to be a requirement for cabin crew. Virgin Atlantic[17] noticed that this was restricting their ability to hire a diverse range of staff. So they kept the requirement but introduced swimming classes between the interview and starting the job.

246. **Help your recruits learn your ways:** When we recruited in 2021 we assumed people would understand how Happy makes online learning truly interactive. But we found that our recruits did not. It wasn't necessarily that they lacked the skills, but they needed to understand the techniques that enable a fully interactive online session.

So we put every recruit through a two-hour session on how to make Zoom interactive, before bringing them to interview. As a result we recruited far more people and from more diverse backgrounds.

247. **Hire for kindness:** "Don't hire for qualifications. We can teach them that. But we can't teach them to be kind and compassionate and to care. We find that out through scenarios,

through discussions, trying to use more of those happy approaches." Katherine Horler, Chief Executive, Adviza

248. **Qualifications often test the wrong stuff:** It is not just degrees, but all qualifications. At Happy we employed a young woman at the age of 16, who had no GCSEs at all. Three years later she became Finance Manager. And in all her time in that role she never had to calculate the angle on a triangle or solve a quadratic equation or do any of the other stuff involved in a Maths GCSE.

Induction

You've recruited your new star. How do you make sure every part of their induction works for them and works for you?

249. **Send them champagne:** One company described how they really want their new staff to feel valued. So a week before they arrive they send them a bottle of champagne and a pair of champagne glasses.

250. **Send them flowers or a plant:** At Happy, we know that won't be appropriate for everybody. So we send them flowers or a plant, again to make them feel appreciated.

251. **Just send a card:** "You talked about sending a card and flowers to new recruits before they start. We have a tight budget so we ditched the flowers and just send the card. It's a small gesture but it makes a real difference." Katherine Horler, Chief Executive, Adviza

252. **Use your fresh eyes:** "New staff can be a revelation. I search them out and ask what they've spotted, what doesn't seem right – before they've become too acclimatised." Nikki Gatenby, CEO, Propellernet

253. **A little black book:** "At every company since Rackspace, I'd give all new joiners a little black book. They were asked to write down anything they noticed that was annoying or stupid about the way we worked. I'd then meet them for lunch regularly during their first six months to discuss their ideas for change or improvement." ["F**k Plan B", Dom Monkhouse]

254. **Stop the inductions:** "We stopped inducting people. Instead we got them to meet with their colleagues to share what you need to do to succeed and survive." Derek Hill, MD, ATS

Promotion

255. **At WL Gore people promote themselves:** When John Housego was asked, at the 2016 Happy Workplaces Conference, how people got promoted at W. L. Gore his answer was: "People step up and take on extra commitments.

"So because we take our own commitments we can promote ourselves every day, every year, at every opportunity. You've got to balance that around the whole work/life balance and whether you can deliver it or not, but self-promotion is how we grow in Gore and actually one of our core beliefs is a freedom principle: freedom to grow and develop and help others to grow and develop."

256. **At Happy we didn't replace the Managing Director:** When the Managing Director of our IT training business left, we, influenced by the Gore example, decided not to replace him. Instead, I said to staff, "If you want to take on one of his responsibilities, go for it." A range of people stepped up to take on activities, while some of his tasks simply didn't continue. At the next salary panel, people were rewarded for the tasks they took on.

257. **Let people choose their job title:** Or have no job titles, as W. L. Gore does.

Moving people on

In *The Happy Manifesto* I describe the example of McKinsey: when they know somebody isn't going to make Partner, they encourage them to leave. But they give them several months and often find them work with one of their clients. As a result their ex-employees are devoted fans rather than disgruntled and resentful.

258. **Help people leave:** "If somebody isn't working out, help them to find what they want. We helped somebody leave and set up as a holistic therapy consultant. Now they come back and provide massages to our staff." Chris May, Director, Mayden

259. **Get rid of the a**holes:** "We just wanted team players in the Ministry of Social Security. We asked the a**holes to move to the Finance Ministry." Laurence Vanhee, Belgian Ministry of Social Security

When one of your people leaves, how can you ensure that they leave with a good impression, so that they will promote your organisation to others?

260. **When people quit:** I used to dread the arrival of an unpostmarked white envelope on my desk. It would normally be somebody's resignation.

Now at Happy we encourage people to let us know if they are thinking of leaving. That helps us to plan, though we still involve them in any big projects, and avoids sudden departures.

261. **A farewell meal for those leaving:** When a person leaves CC&R, team members join together for a meal with the person who is leaving. "Everybody comes prepared with a personal story about that person's time with the organization," explains Frederick Laloux. "Of course, the stories are meant to celebrate the person who is leaving." [*Reinventing Organisations*, Frederick Laloux]

262. **The company that never fires people for poor performance:** Several years ago, Next Jump founder Charlie Kim said that he regarded his employees as family. One responded by

asking if he would fire a member of his family if they behaved badly. Charlie came in the next day and announced that, from then on, nobody would be fired from Next Jump for poor performance.

"It has had some unintended consequences," explained Tarun Gidoomal, London Managing Director. "First, it means you have to be very careful in who you hire. Virtually the whole team now has to agree before we appoint somebody as we know it's a job for life. Second, people have opened up more, and been prepared to share their stories, their faults and failures because there is no risk of getting fired. And it's led to people being more prepared to take healthy business risks."

263. **Have a "stay interview":** Exit interviews are really useful, and often lead you to become aware of issues. However it can be too late by then.

Instead try a stay interview, where you can deal with an issue before they have to leave.

Case Study: Toyota

"We build people before we build cars"

Despite its huge size, Toyota still includes many of the principles discussed in this chapter, including freedom to innovate, celebrating mistakes, hiring for attitude. The Toyota Production System has made it one of the most innovative companies on the planet.

12 ways that Toyota creates a great workplace

After visiting the Toyota engine plant in Deeside I wrote these reflections:

264. **More people, fewer machines:** The first surprise was that the assembly line was not full of robots. Most of the machinery looked as if it could have been in place 30 years ago. We were told that they have actually **reduced** the level of automation in recent years. "People are more flexible than machines" was one response.

There was also no SAP (Systems Analysis Program) or ERP (Enterprise Resource Planning) system in evidence. Instead the key monitoring tool was developed in Excel. "We want a system that adapts to the way we work, not to have to adapt to the way an existing piece of software works." And this was no paperless office. Charts and written sheets were everywhere.

265. **Two improvements from each member every month:** "Never be satisfied with what you have got" is a core principle at Toyota. Every "member" (as staff are called) is expected to come up with two "kaizens" (or ideas for improvement) each month. Indeed they are trained in fabrication and welding to enable them to be able to test out their ideas.

Time is dedicated to kaizen: each member is allocated 15 minutes a day to identify possible improvements. Managers will try and avoid opposing a change, even if it has been tried before and not worked. A key point of kaizen is personal development: "The learning comes from the journey".

266. **Intrinsic motivation, not money:** There are no rewards for any financial gain resulting from the improvements people make. "We don't want our people driven by money but by the desire to improve the process." There are also no individual bonuses, only collective bonuses.

267. **Standardise then improve:** There is a sense of empowerment and engagement wherever you go at Toyota. But there is no sense of anarchy. Every process is carefully documented. "Every member is encouraged to improve the current process, but that standardisation makes it easy to return to the old process if the idea doesn't work." If the idea works, then the new approach is standardised and written down as a process by the member who created the improvement.

"Without standardisation there can be no kaizen," said Toyota founder Taiichi Ohno.

268. **Each Toyota assembly line is different:** When a new engine is created, or a new car rolled out, each plant will be equipped with the same assembly line and set of standardised processes. However each plant is continually innovating and, although yokoten (sharing) means many innovations get adopted at other plants, some don't. The expectation that every member is continually seeking improvement means that every Toyota assembly line is different. There is standardisation of processes on each line but there seems to be no desire for standardisation across sites.

The plant I visited on Deeside had a slightly old-fashioned look to it. But this is apparently the most productive Toyota assembly line on the planet, being the first to achieve an engine every 48 seconds.

269. **Small changes matter:** A kaizen doesn't have to be huge. One example was a lever that popped up a screw, meaning the member didn't need to bend down to pick it up. It was estimated to save two-tenths of a second.

"We build ten million cars a year. Save two-tenths of a second on each one and that's a gain of 560 person hours."

270. **Quality Control Circles: full involvement:** Twice a month the assembly lines shut down for half an hour as every member gathers into their QCCs (Quality Control Circles). Here they study the data and learn more about what is going on in their section and throughout the company.

This may result in further improvements but "that is not the point. The aim is development" and that is what the carefully laid out QCC plans focus on.

271. **A no blame culture:** "We would never blame the individual. If something goes wrong, it is the process that has gone wrong." One of the two key pillars of the Toyota system is jidoka. Every member can pull a cord to stop the belt if there is an issue, to help eliminate the root cause of problems.

Team leaders must never criticise a member for pulling the cord. "We want them to pull the cord." "If you blame somebody for failure, all that will happen is people will start sweeping problems under the carpet."

272. **Systems to prevent error:** I knew that W. Edwards Deming (the US management theorist who had such an influence on Japanese methods) was clear that errors are caused by processes, not by people. But visiting a Toyota assembly line really showed what he meant. Members will repeat the same process 150 times in a two-hour session. It would be easy to miss a step or use the wrong part if the process allowed it.

The member we watched was working alternately on different engines with different spark plugs. If both types of spark plugs were available and the member picked the wrong set, that would not be "human error" but process error. So a plastic shield swings across between the two sets so only the correct one is uncovered. As backup (in case the shield fails) a green light goes on over the correct set of plugs. It is almost impossible to accidentally use the wrong plugs.

It is all fairly low-tech, but these are simple systems that prevent human error by making it as difficult as possible to make that error. This is known as "poka-yoke" or "mistake-proofing" and is intrinsic to the Toyota approach. If your system allows somebody to make a mistake, it is the system that is wrong, not the person.

> 94% of problems in business are systems-driven
> and only 6% are people-driven.
> Attributed to W. Edwards Deming

273. **It's all about the people:** "Our greatest resource is flexible, motivated members." Respect for people sits alongside continuous improvement at the core of the Toyota Way. "When you hire two hands you get a brain free. Clever people we have here."

Managers are there to support. The development of the members is the most important thing you can do. "We build people before we build cars."

In the standard management diagram, the front-line staff are at the bottom and the top managers are at the top. At Toyota it is the other way round, clearly stating that the role of managers is to support their members. They are expected to coach them and to ask "what can I do to help?"

274. **Recruit for attitude, train for skills:** "We can train people in the skills they need." They recruit for good communication, teamwork and willingness to improve. "It is not that they have the best skills but the right team fit."

275. **Get them to do the job in the recruitment process:** Those who know me will know this is my core requirement for effective recruitment. But Toyota take it to an extra level. Before they are invited to interview, applicants must spend a full day on an assembly line. Not the real one, but a mock assembly line. They are even asked to come up with one or two kaizen improvements at the end of it.

"We used to have people quitting on their first day, when they realised what they had to do. We don't get that any more. If they are not up to it, they quit on that mock day."

276. **It's about people, not money:** One visitor asks if they have costed the time "lost" in working on kaizen and Quality Control Circles, if they have compared it to the benefits that result and if they can show it makes financial sense.

The Toyota representative looks slightly baffled. It is one of those moments when you see two people working from completely different assumptions. It seems this is a calculation that Toyota would never see the need to carry out.

"We will never focus purely on cost," he explains. "Development of the members is the most important thing you can do, our biggest resource."

I left feeling that Toyota is truly a remarkable workplace. Those twin pillars of respect for people and continuous improvement seem genuine and embedded in everything they do.

The visit was part of the excellent Onsite Insights visits programme.[18] Do contact them to find how you can get first-hand experience of great companies (including Happy).

6. Celebrate Mistakes

One of the things people like best at Happy is that they know if they try something new, possibly stretch themselves, and they do their best then they will never be blamed if it goes wrong. Indeed, a no-blame culture seems to be a feature of many of the most innovative organisations in the world.

> "Mistakes (WSTMSUW, whoever screws the most stuff up wins) are regularly celebrated (not 'tolerated') as essential steps on the path to progress; one successful CEO-innovator says he owes his success to a three-word motto: 'Fail. Forward. Fast.'"
>
> *The Excellence Dividend*, Tom Peters

277. **Celebrate with wine and cheese:** Michael Davies, Head of Sales at Macquarie Telecom, told me of when he'd recently hired a yacht. He was told, "If you get stuck on a sandbank call us out, and we will arrive with a bottle of wine and a cheese platter to celebrate."

Did he have to call them out? "Yes, twice." Both times the wine and cheese were brought. The reason was simple: getting stuck on a sandbank isn't a problem if you know how to get off. If you don't, then you could wreck the underside of the boat. If something does go wrong, it's great to make sure that whoever fixes it is the best person to fix it.

278. **Intuit: "We celebrate failure":** Accounting software company Intuit gives a special award for the Best Failure and holds "failure parties". "At Intuit we celebrate failure," explains co-founder Scott Cook, "because every failure teaches something important that can be the seed for the next great idea."

279. **Hold a party to celebrate:** Huntsman is a chemical company with a plant in north-east England. On the wall there used to be a big red button which, if pressed, discharged the

chemicals into the local river. One day the scaffolders were in, and one of them nudged the button with his pole. His scaffolding company sacked him. But, when Huntsman found out, they insisted he be reinstated, sent back to work for them and even held a party to celebrate.

Nobody saw him press the button, but he had taken responsibility and gone to the control room to let them know. As a result it could be fixed in 30 minutes, rather than 24 hours; there was minimal environmental damage and no fine. "Holding that party sent a message round, and it spread like wildfire, that Huntsman is a no-blame culture." If problems result from a mistake, it is rarely the mistake that causes them. More often, it is the cover-up.

280. **Praise people when they own up to a mistake:** This is crucial. Make a point of warmly praising or celebrating when somebody owns up to a mistake.

> "[Management guru] Peter Drucker provocatively suggested that businesses should find all the employees who never make mistakes and fire them because employees who never make mistakes never do anything interesting."
> *Leading with Happiness*, Alexander Kjerulf

281. **Gore celebrates failure with beer or champagne:** W. L. Gore, the makers of Goretex, was once voted the most innovative company in the US. They have long celebrated when a project doesn't work with beer or champagne – "just as they would if it had been a success."

Gore's fundamental beliefs include: "Action is prized; ideas are encouraged; and making mistakes is viewed as part of the creative process."

> "If we're not making mistakes, we're not trying hard enough."
> James Quincey, CEO, Coca Cola

282. **Menlo Innovations "make mistakes faster":** This is a core principle at Menlo, the software company that founder Richard Sheridan set up to create a joyful work environment.

As my colleague Alex Kjerulf puts it, "They know that mistakes are an integral part of doing anything cool and interesting and the sooner you can screw up, the sooner you can learn and move on."

283. **Netflix wants more failures:** Netflix CEO Reed Hastings has worried that they have too many hit shows and not enough failures. Speaking at the 2017 Code Conference, he said, "I'm always pushing the content team. We have to take more risk.

"You have to try more crazy things, because we should have a higher cancel rate overall." *Business Insider*, "Netflix CEO Reed Hastings wants to start cancelling more shows — here's why".[19]

284. **Reward failure at Google:** Google's Head of People Operations, Laszlo Bock, states: "It's also important to reward failure" so as to encourage risk-taking. Bock gives the example of Google Wave, an online platform launched in 2010 and closed a year later. "They took a massive, calculated risk. And failed. So we rewarded them." [Work Rules. Laszlo Bock]

285. **Five thousand failures:** James Dyson says he made 5,127 prototypes of his vacuum cleaner before he got it right. That means 5,126 were failures.

> "If your goals are ambitious and crazy enough, even failure will be a pretty good achievement."
> Larry Page, Google Founder, in *Work Rules*, Laszlo Bock

286. **Tata: "Failure is a gold mine":** Rajan Tata, founder and chairman of Indian conglomerate Tata, created a prize for the Best Failed Idea as he neared retirement. The aim is to spark innovation and keep the company from avoiding risks.

"Failing Well" is a programme at Smith College, Massachusetts: "What we're trying to teach is that failure is not a bug of learning, it's the feature," explained Rachel Simmons, who runs the initiative. On enrolment, students receive a Certificate of Failure that declares they are "hereby authorized to screw up, bomb, or fail" at a relationship, a project, a test, or any other initiative that seems hugely important and "still be a totally worthy, utterly excellent human being". *New York Times*, "On Campus, Failure Is on the Syllabus".[20]

Celebrate at the Church of Fail: At Brighton-based social media company Nixon McInnes the Church of Fail was a monthly ritual. Employees are invited to stand and confess their mistakes, and are wildly applauded for doing so. "Making failure socially acceptable makes us more open and creative," said CEO Will McInnes.

> "If people tell me they skied all day and never fell down, I tell them to try a different mountain."
> Michael Bloomberg, Founder of Bloomberg

287. **Experimental culture at Next Jump:** "We try stuff out," explains Tarun Gidoomal. "Some of it works and a lot of it doesn't. To be honest, 60% of what we have done has failed. We have a saying that there are no mistakes ... only lessons learnt."

288. **Own up to your mistakes:** Dom Monkhouse explains how, at Rackspace, if they screwed something up, they would immediately call the customer. "Most companies don't because they think admitting failure will erode customers' trust. But for Rackspace, the opposite happened. Customers trusted us more because we were honest." [Mind Your F**king Business, Dom Monkhouse]

289. **Of course we are not sure:** Feike Sijbesma, former CEO of Dutch company Royal DSM, explains, "When we did daring things my Board asked, 'Are you sure?' My answer was, 'Of course not, there's no way to be sure.' We created a culture to be open about having insecurities, but also to have the guts and determination to go after the opportunities." [CEO Excellence, Carolyn Dewar, Scott Keller, and Vikram Malhotra]

290. **I got it wrong:** Be prepared to say, "I got it wrong, it was my fault."

> "We don't make mistakes at WD-40 Company, we have 'learning moments', a positive or negative outcome of any situation that is openly and freely shared to benefit all."
>
> Garry Ridge, CEO, WD-40

Case Study: Google

Some will regard Google as a controversial example. We know that it does not pay its fair share of taxes, and is seen as a key part of "surveillance capitalism", monitoring our every move. There have also been staff protests in recent years, and they have recently laid off 12,000 staff despite making a $66 billion profit.

However, it has regularly won "best place to work" surveys, both in the United States and internationally. And it is clear that the founders, Sergey Brin and Larry Page, set it up with the belief that success would result from an empowered and fulfilled workforce.

291. **How Google founder Larry Page learnt the importance of freedom at work:** Kim Scott explains a key influence on the founder's approach: "Shortly after I joined Google, Larry Page told me about a time when he'd had a boss who was suspicious of ambition. While on a summer internship, Larry had been given an assignment that would have taken him a couple of days if he'd been given the freedom to do it his way. He explained the advantages of his approach to the boss, but the boss would have none of it: he insisted that Larry do it 'the way they'd always done it'."

Instead of two days, Larry was forced to spend all summer working on the project. The wasted time and effort were pure torture for him. Like most of us, Larry discovered that a boss who held him back could make life miserable. 'Three months of my life wasted and gone forever. I never want anyone at Google to have a boss like that. Ever.'" [Radical Candour, Kim Scott]

292. **Being the boss doesn't mean you can tell people what to do:** "Decisions really didn't get made by authority at Google – not even by the founders," explains Kim Scott in *Radical Candour*. "At one point, Google's engineers decided to redesign the AdWords front end to make it easier for advertisers to choose different kinds of ad formats. Since most of Google's revenue came from AdWords, it was important to get this right. In one meeting, I

watched Google co-founder Sergey Brin try to persuade a team of engineers to try his solution to the challenge of presenting to advertisers all the choices they had – different kinds of ad formats, different ways to make sure their ads showed up when and where they wanted, etc. – in the simplest possible way.

"The team proposed a different solution from Sergey's. He suggested that they put a couple of people working on his approach and let the rest of the team pursue their favoured solution. The team refused. Sergey, in a rare burst of frustration, banged the table and said, 'If this were an ordinary company, you'd all be doing it my way. I just want a couple of people to try my idea!' He was clearly exasperated, but his grin showed that he was also proud of having built a team that would stand up to him. In the end, the team convinced him that theirs was the better way."

> "Workplaces that permit employees more freedom tap into that natural intrinsic motivation, which in turn helps employees feel even more autonomous and capable."
> *Work Rules*, Laszlo Bock, Head of People, Google

293. **At Google, people set their own targets:** Yvonne Agyei, then Google Head of Benefits, made clear at the 2013 Happy Workplaces Conference that the Google approach is to let people set their own targets, within the overall goals. Every quarter the corporate strategy is revealed for the next three months.

"As a manager it is not your role to tell your people what they should be doing, rather it's a bottom-up process. Each Googler is expected to understand what the corporate objectives are and figure out how they contribute." Within three weeks of the whole-company objectives being set, every one of the then 38,000 members of staff had set their own OKRs (Objectives and Key Results), which means they each determined what they would be doing for the quarter.

294. **At Google, targets are visible to all:** In the Google directory, right next to a person's email and phone number are their OKR targets. This means, when contacting somebody, you can find out what their focus is and consider how what you want fits with that.

295. **Weekly Town Hall meetings at Google:** Every week Sergey and Larry hold TGIF (Thank God It's Friday), where they personally talk with hundreds of Googlers at the Mountain View HQ and thousands worldwide. They explain upcoming product launches, and share information on what the company is doing. Plus they take questions and "pretty much nothing is off limits". Googlers use simple online technology to vote questions up and down and decide what gets asked.

296. **Restrict what managers can do:** "We deliberately take power and authority over employees away from managers. Here is a sample of the decisions managers at Google cannot make unilaterally: whom to hire; whom to fire; how someone's performance is rated; how much of a salary increase, bonus, or stock grant to give someone; who is selected to win an award for great management; whom to promote; when code is of sufficient quality to be incorporated into our software code base; the final design of a product and when to launch it." [Work Rules, Laszlo Bock]

297. **Give people time to explore:** In *Work Rules*, Laszlo Bock describes how, for 65 years, 3M has offered its employees 15% of their time to explore – based on the core belief that creativity needs freedom. Products include Post-It notes and a clever abrasive material called Trizact, which somehow sharpens itself as it's used.

"Our version is 20 percent time, meaning that engineers have 20 percent of their week to focus on projects that interest them, outside of their day jobs but presumably still related to Google's work." (Note: there is some dispute about how much this is still in place and it does seem only to apply to engineers.)

> "What managers miss is that every time they give up a little control, it creates a wonderful opportunity for their team to step up, while giving the manager herself more time for new challenges."
>
> Laszlo Bock, Head of People, Google in *Work Rules*

298. **Google's dress code:** CEO Eric Schmidt was once asked at a company meeting what the Google dress code was. "You must wear something," was his answer. [Eric Schmidt, How Google Works]

7. Community: Create Mutual Benefit

What resources and skills do your people have that could have a real benefit to others? Creating mutual benefit helps the community but also can help your people.

299. **Supporting coding in local schools:** Every branch of Next Jump is asked to adopt a local non-profit organisation. A particular focus is on schools. The New York office adopted PS119 in South Bronx, a school where 75% of the kids live below the poverty line.

They funded the re-opening of the after-school programme (at a cost of $300,000 a year) to enable parents to continue to do their jobs uninterrupted, allow teachers to earn extra income and give students the extra support to grow and learn. Next Jumpers have been participating directly in the programme, with every employee in the New York office spending a day a month helping to build and teach a curriculum.

> "A company that can't figure out how to run their business in a way that makes the world better and happier shouldn't be in business at all."
> *Leading with Happiness*, Alexander Kjerulf]

300. **Use your core skills to help:** With "Code for a cause" at Next Jump, three people can take two weeks out to scale and build a charitable project. One member of staff had a relation who had been in juvenile prison. She got together with two colleagues and spent the two weeks building tools for a charity helping ex-offenders.

301. **Serve the wider community:** The second biggest source of recruitment at Timpson, after staff recommendation, is prison. The company not only recruits from people leaving prison, but has workshops within prisons to train up people for when they leave. They have recruited over 300 ex-prisoners. John Timpson: "We

have 40 staff, including nine branch managers, who are still in prison – on day release."

> "I hired a corporate social responsibility person several years before I hired a sales person."
> *Things a Little Bird Told Me*, Biz Stone

Seven crucial tests

302. **Positive contribution:** Does your product or service make a positive contribution to society?

303. **Community:** Does your company contribute to the community?

304. **Employees:** Do you treat your staff well and help them fulfil their potential?

305. **Salaries:** Are you paying a decent wage (in the UK, at least the Real Living Wage)?

306. **Suppliers:** Do you pay your suppliers within 30 days, especially local traders and small businesses?

307. **Taxes:** Do you pay your taxes, and make a contribution to society?

308. **Climate crisis:** Are you heading towards net zero?

If you can't answer "Yes" to these seven questions, then the fact that you might contribute 1% of profit to charity is an irrelevance.

309. **Purpose-driven companies perform better:** Socially conscious and purpose-driven companies featured by Babson College Professor Raj Sisodia in his book *Firms of Endearment* have outperformed the S&P 500 by a staggering 14 times over a period of 15 years, 10 of which were after the publication of the book. [Brave New Work, Aaron Dignan]

310. **Are you a B Corp?:** The B Corp movement is based on organisations with a purpose beyond profit. B Corps are based on an extensive survey, which test whether they make a positive contribution to society.

Case Study: Haier

Haier is a Chinese white goods manufacturer employing 80,000 people, based on a non-hierarchical approach. It was introduced at the Thinkers50 London 2019 Conference as "possibly the most innovative company on the planet". Corporate Rebels have described it as "The world's most pioneering company of our times".[21]

Haier has been described as "addicted to change". Over 30 years, Zhang Ruimin, the CEO, has led the company thorough five strategic cycles of change, each transforming the culture of the organisation.

"We replaced the bureaucratic model with a model based on self-employment, self-motivation, and self-organization", explained Zhang. "Our goal is to let everyone become their own CEO."

Haier uses the concept of RenDanHeYi. Rendanheyi is a management philosophy that prioritizes individual employees and customers, encouraging employee entrepreneurship and a customer-centric approach.

"Ren" refers to the employees; ""Dan" represents empowering individuals within the organization to act as entrepreneurs, take ownership of their work, and make independent decisions.; and "Heyi" emphasizes finding solutions that create value for all parties involved.

Zhang took over as General Manager of the Qingdao Refrigerator Plant in 1984, when it was close to bankruptcy. With a determination to focus on quality, one of his first acts has gone down in company legend.

311. **Defective fridges**: After receiving a customer complaint about a defective fridge, he discovered 76 of the fridges at the plant had the same problem. He had them brought together in the

Allowing workers to destroy defects can help them understand the impact it has

centre of the factory, gave sledgehammers to the workers and had them destroy the faulty fridges (each then worth two years' salary for a typical Chinese worker).

The aim was to make clear that quality was not optional.

312. **Stunned fish:** He expanded the company by buying up 18 rivals in a strategy called "revitalising stunned fish" (the stunned fish being loss-making companies with poor leadership). He has continued this approach on the international stage, one of Haier's latest acquisitions being General Electric Appliances.

313. **Empowering employees:** Since being taken over by Haier, General Electric Appliances has had double-digit growth. They did this by "empowering employees and creating value for customers". This approach involves breaking down silos within the company and encouraging collaboration across departments to improve innovation and speed up decision-making.

314. **Product not profit:** Haier's leadership did not force RenDanHeYi on GE Appliances. It did begin educating it about the new model but believed that local people know best what works locally.

Kevin Nolan was appointed as CEO of GE Appliances. Previously GE had generally made a finance-oriented MBA its CEO, but Haier wanted a technologist in charge to focus on products rather than profits. HBR, 2023, "How Chinese Companies Are Reinventing Management".[22]

315. **Self-organising teams of 8:** Speaking at the Thinkers50 Conference in London in 2019, Zhang explained that Haier had split its 80,000 staff into units of 8. Instead of needing 13 levels of approval to spend, they now decide for themselves.

316. **Zero approval:** "Without management things are working out much better. Zero signature, zero approval." Growth went from 8% to 30% when they got rid of management.

317. **Can you give up these three things:** Zhang was asked if any company can follow the Haier model? "Only if the CEO is prepared to give up three things: hiring and firing; salaries; making decisions. Are you prepared to trust your people?"

318. **Zero distance to the customer:** Crucial to Haier's approach is a focus on the customer, with the company's key platform being open to customers. As Zhang puts it: "In the past, employees waited to hear from the boss. Now, they listen to the customer."

319. **Remove the managers:** As Haier moved towards its RenDanHeYi approach, it abolished the roles of 12,000 middle managers, who had to either become entrepreneurs or leave. There are now only two layers of management between the CEO and front-line employees.

8. Love Work, Get a Life

The world, and your job, needs you well rested, well nourished and well supported.

Improve your life balance

320. **Put the phone down:** "Average working hours have increased by 27% since we put emails on the phone. So put the phone away and stop using it for email." Nikki Gatenby, Propellernet

> "No distraction leads to quiet, quiet leads to flow, flow leads to progress, progress leads to satisfaction."
> Bruce Daisley, *The Joy of Work*

321. **The wellbeing of your staff is important:** "John Lewis had a free-at-the-point-of-service medical system for its partners [its staff] 20 years before the NHS was created." Sarah Gillard, Director, John Lewis Partnership

322. **Leave your laptop at the office:** Although rated as a great place to work, Google has a notoriously long-hours culture. However even at Google, there are attempts to get people to work less and avoid burn-out. Laszlo Bock explains how Google Dublin's People department introduced "Dublin goes dark", encouraging people to leave at 6pm, and providing drop-off locations for laptops to prevent people working in the evening at home.

He quotes People Operations leader Helen Tynan: "Lots of people chatted the next day about what they had done, and how long the evening had seemed with lots of time for doing things." The idea spread from the People department to the whole of Google Dublin and has now gone international. [Work Rules, Laszlo Bock]

323. **Finish at 5.30 even if you are the top guy in the military:** "Millions of Americans have given their country outstanding

service," Harry Truman once said, "[but] General of the Army George Marshall gave it victory."

Despite being responsible for the outcome of World War II, Marshall insisted on leaving the office at 5.30pm and relaxing in the evening. If this vital job could be done within work hours, why do others need to work long hours? [A World Without Email, Cal Newport]

> "Leaders who can't do their jobs in a regular 40-hour work week must be either incredibly unproductive, bad at managing their time, or terrible at delegating."
> [Leading with Happiness, Alexander Kjerulf]

324. **Commute by bicycle, not car:** It will make you happier and reduce your risk of a heart attack by 24%, and give you a 20% lower risk of death overall. And it helps the environment. (Check Here)

325. **Keep 50% of your time unscheduled:** Do you have meetings and activities throughout your day? When do you have spare time for people? Tom Peters suggests in Extreme Humanism: "Every leader should routinely keep a substantial portion of his or her time – I would say as much as 50 percent – unscheduled."

326. **Time for Rachel:** "My PA sets aside 'Time for Rachel' in my diary. That is time when I'm not meeting anybody, just taking time to reflect." Rachel Street, CEO, Heart of Kent Hospice

327. **If Jeff can do it:** "I want to tell you a story about a guy called Jeff. Back in 1994, Jeff left the long hours of a highly paid corporate career on Wall Street to start his own business. But Jeff doesn't like to work too hard. He goes to bed early, gets eight hours' sleep and, after waking up, likes to 'putter' a while, enjoying his morning coffee, reading the newspaper, cooking big breakfasts and hanging out with his kids before they go to school. After breakfast, he does the dishes before starting work at 10am.

"Jeff realized a few years ago that he works best in the mornings, so he likes to get any 'high IQ' meetings done and dusted before lunchtime. Jeff is well aware that, due to decision fatigue, making good choices gets harder throughout the day so, by 5pm, he'll postpone any decision-making until 10am the next day. Try to picture Jeff, and you might think of a relaxed entrepreneur, with plenty of time for his friends and family, perhaps running a lifestyle business or small consultancy. It's unlikely you'll have pictured Jeff Bezos. If Jeff Bezos can make billions and enjoy his life, why are you sacrificing so much?" [The Hard Work Myth by Barnaby Lashbrooke]

328. **Avoid a long-hours culture:** Set an example of working to your hours and taking time off. The evidence is clear, long hours do not work. Your customers want your people relaxed, well rested and nourished.

A study at Stanford University[23] found that hours decline sharply when a person works more than 50 hours a week, and after 55 productivity drops so much that there is no benefit to it.

329. **Just four hours a day:** In approximately four hours' work a day, Charles Darwin wrote 19 books including *The Descent of Man* and *On the Origin of Species*. The rest of the time, he went for walks, had a nap, that kind of thing. [Rest, Alex Soojung-Kim Pang]

Health and wellbeing

Is health and wellbeing a key element in your work culture?

330. **Make exercise part of the culture:** At Next Jump all staff are encouraged to go to the gym twice a week, and supported to eat healthily. And the dance battle, mentioned above certainly helps too.

They have a fitness competition where every Next Jumper is put into one of five fitness teams. The team that collectively exercises the most in any given week receives a monetary incentive, which is split between the team. "We went from 25% of the company working out twice a week to 95%!"

331. **3pm exercise:** Every day at 3pm at Happy work stops for staff (or those who want to) to do some stretching and core-building exercises. Started by Nicole Martin, then our newest member of staff, the options are chosen from a hat full of exercise ideas. It has become a very popular break.

332. **Give yourself "me time":** what do you really enjoy doing?

333. **Help your people find "me time":** Encourage everyone to do what they really enjoy.

334. **Quiet space:** Create a quiet area where an individual is trusted, respected and allowed to just be for a while.

Taking time to reflect

Imagine you are in the woods and see a woodcutter with a blunt saw. You say to them, "You could get so much more cut down if you sharpened your saw." They say: "Do you see how many trees I have to cut down? I haven't got time to sharpen my saw."

Do you find time to sharpen your saw?

335. **Time to reflect:** If you take 15 minutes to reflect at the end of the day, you can improve your productivity by 22.8%. That's the conclusion of a study at Harvard Business School.[24] Participants spent 15 minutes writing in a journal to embed their learning from the day, and produced these dramatic results.

Spending 15 minutes at the end of the day to reflect on your learning can improve productivity

336. **Walk in the woods with your dog:** One headteacher from Hillingdon described to me how every Monday morning – in school time – she goes for a two-hour walk in the woods with her dog. "In terms of the thinking I get done, it is the most productive part of my working week."

337. **10 days a year at home:** Another headteacher, this time from Gloucestershire, told me how they got their governors to agree to them spending 10 days a year, during school term-times, at home. They would then use this time to think about how to improve the school's processes and ways of working, or develop strategies for the school.

338. **Morning and afternoon "Fika":** In Sweden it is standard practice to take a 15-minute break for tea and cakes, normally at 10am and 3pm. "Every company I have worked in has taken Fika twice a day," says Annie Hagman, Swedish nurse

339. **Book in innovation time:** One thing we learnt from doing this at Happy was that, if you want innovation and creativity, you have to set aside the time for it. It has to be booked in. So every month our key people on our leadership programmes come together for three hours to look at what can be improved. It means our delivery is continually changing and improving.

340. **Break your arm:** As I worked with one group of NHS leaders, many described how they had no time in their hectic schedules to reflect. Then one surgeon mentioned that, a couple of years previously, he had broken his arm. For three months he couldn't work in the operating theatre. Instead he used the time to look at their processes and came up with new ways of working that resulted in efficiencies way beyond that three months in benefit. Don't wait to break your arm – can you find the time?

341. **Put people to work on improvement:** A partner in a GP surgery in Exeter described how they took over an underperforming surgery. Everybody felt overworked and lacked any spare time to think about how to improve the service.

"So we worked out who were the most creative people, best able to come up with new approaches. And we deliberately timetabled innovation time for them, even in what felt a very hectic schedule. The core question was 'what are GPs (our most expensive resource) doing that other people could do?'". She went on to list a dozen improvements that this had led to, resulting in less pressure and actually improving the service to patients.

342. **Take a break in a café:** Most mornings, on my cycle into work, I stop in a café for a hot chocolate. I spend that time either getting some writing done (yep, I'm in a café right now) or taking time to reflect before heading into the busy office. I often stop off on the way home too (though I do have the benefit of a short, 14-minute commute).

343. **The Twitter boss who set aside two hours a day for reflection:** Kim Scott describes how Dick Costelo, while CEO of Twitter from 2010 to 2015, would schedule two hours' thinking

time into his diary – every day. During this time Twitter grew from 30 million monthly active users to over 300 million. [Radical Candour, Kim Scott]

344. **An hour a day to think:** Peter Drucker, the world-renowned business guru, argued that managers should set aside an hour a day to think. [The Excellence Dividend, Tom Peters]

345. **Find your desert:** "I believe it's important to find a learning space, take time to reflect, e.g. switch off the computer and let your thoughts bubble up. I see it as finding my desert." Adele Paterson, International Health Partners

346. **Set aside time for reflection and development:** "We hold two inset weeks at different parts of the year, purely for staff development. It is worth it." Mervyn Kaye, Youth Works

347. **Find space in the day to be social:** One example is when we banned eating at desks in the Happy office, forcing staff to take a break. Suddenly people got to talk to each other while they ate their lunch.

348. **Reflect together at work:** At German company Heiligenfeld, every Tuesday morning, 350 staff come together and engage in joint reflection. "Employees often credit [this] one practice in particular for making the company an outstanding workplace." [Reinventing Organisations, Frederick Laloux]

349. **Four silent days a year:** Laloux also describes how, once a quarter, Heiligenfeld holds a mindfulness day which both staff and patients spend in silence. "Patients are invited to remain entirely silent (they wear a tag with the word 'silence' to remind each other), while the staff speaks only when needed, in whispers (staff wear a tag with the word 'mindfulness')." [Reinventing Organisations, Frederick Laloux]

350. **Clarity breaks**: "We take 30 mins every week to just think about the team/dept/business and how we can improve," says Matt Smalley, Head of Customer Success, accessplanit.

351. **Performance reviews are better if you take a holiday:** "In the US and Canada ... for each 10 vacation hours a person took, we found on average that performance reviews were 8 percent higher," said Maryella Gockel, Flexibility Strategy leader at EY.[25]

352. **Research shows that taking breaks makes sense:** A Microsoft study found that breaks between meetings allow the brain to "reset". Even two straight hours of meetings can cause stress and reductions in performance. Instead take a 10-minute break between meetings.

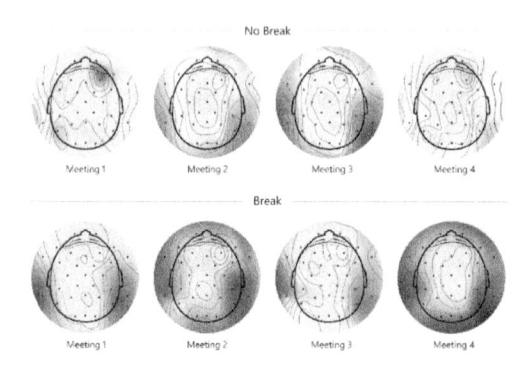

Companies that use mindfulness

353. **Search inside yourself at Google:** It is possible to say that Chade Meng Tan has revolutionised Google: every year, thousands of employees take his mindfulness course Search Inside Yourself. The waiting time for enrolling in the course is over six months. The huge success of the initiative is clear. Tan has managed to convince the scientists and techies at Google, previously suspicious of "hippie stuff", to completely embrace the practices by explaining the neuroscience behind them.

354. **General Mills finds 89% of their leaders become better listeners after mindfulness:** General Mills, the food company behind products such as Old El Paso, Häagen-Dazs and Cheerios, have welcomed the mindfulness revolution and seen their company grow as a result. They reviewed their staff following their seven-week mindfulness and meditation programme: 83% of participants said they took time every day to optimise their productivity, up 23% from before the course; 80% of senior executives reported that they had improved their decision-making process after the course, and 89% said they had become better listeners.

355. **Thousands at Intel practise yoga and mindfulness:** Intel is a company that battles with stress. Lindsey Van Driel commented: "Across the board, every single person we talk to [at Intel] experiences stress ... if they weren't stressed it would mean they're not working hard enough." Intel, 2013. However, inspired by Chade Meng Tan's initiatives at Google, Van Driel decided to do something about it.

Today, thousands of Intel employees have participated in the Awake@Intel programme, which includes yoga and mindfulness practices. Similarly to Google, many of the participants were

Practicing mindfulness can decrease your stress levels and improve creativity

hard-core scientists, initially reporting scepticism towards the benefits of the course. However, after the course the participants reported improved creativity, wellbeing and focus, decreased levels of stress and stronger enthusiasm in projects and meetings.

356. **$9 million saved in healthcare costs after yoga and meditation at Aetna:** Aetna is a medical insurance company and one of the 100 largest firms in the US by revenue. After a near-fatal accident, 58-year-old CEO Mark T. Bertolini decided to drastically transform his company. His measures included a 33% salary increase for the lowest paid employees, and the establishment of free yoga and meditation classes.

These measures have had a huge impact: after the first year, the company reported a whopping $9 million saving in healthcare costs! Moreover, the employees who participated in the classes reported a 28% decrease in stress levels and an increase in productivity levels. These improvements were estimated to be adding a value of about $3,000 per employee a year [Mindful Work, David Gelles]

357. **Feel restored:** "We have been running weekly mindfulness sessions, online, with a lovely lady. I feel really restored after it. Most of the team comes to it." Olivia Clymer, CEO, Healthwatch Central West London

Be productive not busy

Are you productive or are you just busy?

358. **Don't waste time being busy:** "When I discussed with Kirsten Regal, one of Sun's leaders, how little their meeting rooms seemed to be used, she quipped, 'We don't waste time being busy.'" [Reinventing Organisations, Frederick Laloux]

359. **Stop bragging about overwork:** "The people who brag about trading sleep for endless slogs and midnight marathons are usually the ones who can't point to actual accomplishments." [It doesn't have to be crazy at work, Jason Fried and David Heinemeier Hansson]

360. **Monk mode morning:** At least two or three days each week, have no meetings and don't check your inbox before 11am. Instead get stuff done. [The Joy Of Work, Bruce Daisley]

361. **Meeting-free hour at lunchtime:** At Praxis in Bethnal Green no meetings are allowed between 1pm and 2pm. "It helps set boundaries," explains CEO Sally Daglian.

362. **Rate your meetings:** "We had participants indicate on a zero-to-ten scale whether they'd recommend a meeting to a colleague. Was it valuable? After diagnosing the low-scoring ones, we sometimes fixed them but mostly decided that they weren't necessary." Brad Smith, CEO, DBS [*CEO Excellence*, Carolyn Dewar, Scott Keller, and Vikram Malhotra]

363. **Trust-based leaders don't spend their time in meetings:** "When I met Allen Carlson, the CEO of Sun Hydraulics [a publicly listed company], I asked him if he would show me his agenda for the week. He had only four meetings planned in that entire week, two of which were with me." [Reinventing organisations, Frederick Laloux]

364. **No meetings Wednesdays:** "Have no meetings on a Wednesday – no internal or external meetings one day a week," says Matt Smalley, accessplanit.

> "In almost every situation, the expectation of an immediate response is an unreasonable expectation."

365. *It Doesn't Have to be Crazy at Work*, Jason Fried and David Heinemeier Hansson **Reduce meeting time:** Go for 25 minutes (instead of 30), 45 minutes (instead of one hour) or 90 minutes (instead of two hours). You are like to find you get as much done, plus you may get the chance to perform the actions you promised to do before the next meeting.

366. **Cut the meetings:** "I once consulted with a business that had a few employees who were in back-to-back meetings four days a week. The complained they couldn't get any of their work done nor meet their KPIs [Key Performance Indicators]. We freed these employees from needless meetings and their productivity skyrocketed." Dom Monkhouse

[Mind Your F**king Business, Dom Monkhouse]

> "I would tell my staff about the 'dinosaur's tail': As a leader grows more senior, his bulk and tail become huge, but like the brontosaurus, his brain remains modestly small. When plans are changed and the huge beast turns, its tail often thoughtlessly knocks over people and things. That the destruction was unintentional doesn't make it any better."
> *Team of Teams*, Stanley McChrystal

Is it time for a four-day week?

Most people in work feel as if their lives are busy and hectic. Many work long hours. But are we productive? Instead of encouraging long hours at work, some organisations are experimenting with getting people to work less: four days instead of five for the same salary. Some are reducing hours by the full 20%, others are increasing the working day on the remaining four days. Check out the companies below.

Economist John Maynard Keynes famously predicted, back in 1930, that we could all be working just 15 hours per week in the future. In 1926 Henry Ford had introduced the five-day 40-hour working week (cutting weekend working) and found that productivity and profits increased. But reductions in the working week have more or less stalled since then.

The key principle is 100-80-100. You get 100% of the salary for 80% of the time, as long as you are 100% as productive.

367. **Work a short time, rest well and learn a lot:** The 2,300 employees of Microsoft Japan were given Fridays off over the summer of 2019 and found that cutting working hours by 20% resulted in a 40% increase in productivity.[26] It also led to 25% less absence and 23% less use of electricity, with 92% of staff saying they enjoyed the four-day week.

Cutting something out to have a shorter work time, leads to more productivity and happy staff

One key step was apparently to cut meetings to 30 minutes. As CEO Takuya Hirano put it, "Work a short time, rest well and learn a lot."

368. **Perpetual Guardian, 20% productivity increase:** In New Zealand, the finance company Perpetual Guardian moved to a permanent four-day week[27] after a two-month trial. MD Andrew Barnes comments that "Our total profitability, revenue, service standards didn't drop, so as a consequence our productivity must have gone up 20%."

What did change was a reduction in stress, and improvements in work/life balance, loyalty to the firm and employee empowerment. In this TEDx video[28] Andrew explains how the idea was triggered after reading an *Economist* study that found that UK workers only worked productively for 2.5 hours a day.

369. **IIH Denmark, 3 key steps to productivity:** In this 3-minute video,[29] technology company IIH Denmark explain three ways in which they made a four-day week work by finding ways to become more productive:

1) Use the Pomodoro method: These are 25-minute work sprints, where you cannot be disturbed.

2) Set meetings to 20 or 45 minutes, not half an hour or an hour.

3) Decide which work is A (specialist), B (others within the organisation can do) or C (mundane, could be easily outsourced).

370. **Henley Business School: two-thirds reported increases in productivity:** Henley's research, published in a white paper called "Four Better Four Worse",[30] suggests that moving to a four-day week could save businesses £104 billion a year. They found that 34% of business leaders surveyed, and 46% of those in larger businesses, say making the switch to a four-day working week will be "important for future business success". They suggest that we are likely to see more trials in the coming years.

They state that half of all businesses surveyed have enabled a four-day week for some or all of their staff (though not on the basis of four days' work for five days' pay) and claim that £92 billion in savings have already been made.

Benefits of a four-day week

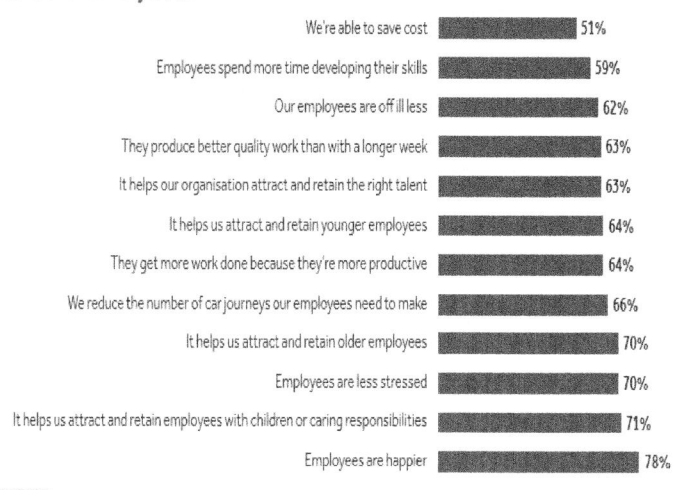

Benefit	%
We're able to save cost	51%
Employees spend more time developing their skills	59%
Our employees are off ill less	62%
They produce better quality work than with a longer week	63%
It helps our organisation attract and retain the right talent	63%
It helps us attract and retain younger employees	64%
They get more work done because they're more productive	64%
We reduce the number of car journeys our employees need to make	66%
It helps us attract and retain older employees	70%
Employees are less stressed	70%
It helps us attract and retain employees with children or caring responsibilities	71%
Employees are happier	78%

371. **Four-day weeks in US schools with one hour longer on the day:** Schools across 21 states are apparently experimenting with a three-day weekend, with an extra hour on the remaining days. Some see this as controversial. It seems that some schools have seen benefits and continued four-day working, while others have switched back to five days.

372. **Could it work in a tech start up?:** South Korea has a notoriously long-hours working week. And tech start-ups are known for working all hours. Bon-Jin runs Woowa Brothers, the Korean equivalent of Deliveroo.

In March 2017 he decided to stop burning the midnight oil and cut hours for all to 35 per week without reducing anyone's pay. "I realised that putting more hours into work didn't lead to higher productivity." Since then, they have grown at >70% a year and sold for $4 billion.

373. **Could it work in healthcare?:** At the Glebe retirement community in Virginia, they moved in 2018 to a trial where nursing assistants received 40 hours of pay for 30 hours of work. They had to hire nine extra staff. However, the $145,023 a year in salary

cost was offset by $122,762 less in hiring cost, overtime and payments to staffing agencies.

Plus, acquired infections dropped 65%, administration of psychoactive medications is down (because nurses spend more time with patients), and staff turnover went from 128% to 44%.

374. **Happy pilot:** Here at Happy we decided to pilot a four-day week for six months, from June to November 2022. The results were interesting. Everybody felt they got as much done in four days as they previously did in five. 77% worked only the 32 hours, while the other 23% worked only one or two hours more.

The key question is whether we are delivering as much value, in terms of customer satisfaction and income, as we were before. Over the period of the pilot our income grew by 20%, with an extra 15% expected next year, with no increase in staff. Our customer satisfaction rose slightly.

375. **Could you try a four-day-week pilot?** Switching completely to a four-day week feels very daunting. However most companies start with a trial of maybe six months. Could your organisation do that? Apparently 63% of Britons support a four-day week,[31] more than in any of the six other European nations surveyed.

Shorter working day or working week

Other alternatives for reducing hours include a six-hour day, a nine-day fortnight or even just going home at 3.30pm on Fridays.

376. **Toyota, Sweden, six-hour shifts are more productive than eight hours:** A Toyota mechanic/dealership in Gothenberg has switched from eight-hour shifts to six hours. Martin Banck explained the approach at Woohoo's Happiness Conference in Copenhagen. (More here).[32]

There was no fall in production and the change led to happier staff, happier customers and more profits. With both shifts able to be fitted into a daytime, costs fell. At the conference, Martin showed a slide on the disadvantages of the shorter day. The slide was blank.

377. **It's Friday, it's 3.30 – go home:** Goodman Masson is a financial recruitment agency, based in London. A couple of summers ago they decided to stop work at 3.30pm on Fridays, enabling staff to enjoy the summer weather and start the weekend early.

"I analysed all the data," explains CEO Guy Hayward, "and it had no effect on the level of sales. We track the phone time of our consultants and this actually went up, as did morale. So we extended it throughout the year. At 3.30pm every Friday I send round an email telling people to go home."

Case Study: W. L. Gore

> "My friends at Fast Company had labelled it as the world's most innovative company, so I thought I should learn more. That first visit was weird, even disconcerting. I found virtually nothing at Gore that matched up with the management practices I had observed in hundreds of other companies – no titles, no bosses and no formal hierarchy.
>
> "I felt like a surgeon who had opened up a patient who looked human, but turned out to be filled with wires and circuits. Yet as I got to know Gore, I realized I had this analogy backwards. Gore was deeply human and by contrast, all those other companies I had studied were cyborgs. Gore's management model seemed wacky only because I had grown accustomed to the inhuman practices that predominated in most other companies."
>
> Gary Hamel, *Wall Street Journal*, 18/3/2000
> (paywall)

WL Gore has been in the Fortune 100 best workplaces list from 1984 to now, one of very few companies to have been placed every year. It has been practising a freedom-based approach for over 50 years.

They are best known as the makers of Goretex, though they have 1,000 products including a wide range of life-saving medical devices. In 2018 they had 9,500 employees and $3.5 billion in sales worldwide. They have regularly been rated as one of the most innovative companies on the planet.

Douglas MacGregor

The enterprise (a word they use instead of company) was set up in 1958 by Bill and Vieve Gore. Bill Gore was heavily influenced by Douglas MacGregor's book *The Human Side of Management*, which posed two management approaches: Theory X (where workers are not trusted) and Theory Y (where they are).

At the time MacGregor said that he'd never actually visited a company that was genuinely based on Theory Y. You could argue that Bill set out to prove that Theory Y could work and built his company on the basis of complete trust.

From the early days the focus was on applying technology to have a meaningful impact on society. Bill Gore wanted to support human fulfilment, embodied in a set of principles and management practices designed to foster trust, initiative and enable the emergence of natural leaders.

W. L. Gore describes itself as an "enterprise" and has leaders, not bosses, and associates, not staff. The nearest equivalent of a manager is a "champion", who the associate chooses. There are no job descriptions. Instead each associate sets down their commitment for the year, a commitment that is regarded very seriously.

378. **Bureaucracy is kept to a minimum:** Teams are self-organising, with generally around 8–10 people. "You get bigger than that, it's not a small team, it's a bigger team, then you've got other problems," explained John Housego, then Business Process Leader at W. L. Gore, at the 2016 Happy Workplaces Conference.

379. **"If you want to be a leader, you'd better find some followers":** At W. L. Gore, you don't get appointed from above. John Housego explained how he had come to run the UK manufacturing plant. "I'd been there three years when the plant manager called me into his office and said 'John, I'm off to the States for nine months, I've asked the team, they want you to lead the plant.'"

John thought he lacked the experience. The response: "Well the team think you can, and that's all that matters."

380. **You don't get promoted at Gore, you step up:** When asked how you get promoted at W. L. Gore, John explained that at Gore "promotion is decided by yourself. You take on extra commitments, you take ownership for something else. That is promotion."

381. **The Freedom Principle:** John explains: "The Freedom Principle at W. L. Gore is the freedom to grow and develop and help others to grow and develop. So we are not going to stop anybody going outside the department and contributing in another team. Even if it's not directly related to their day job. Because they are growing and developing and learning. Though we will hold them to their core job and to their Commitment."

382. **You choose your manager:** I have often described Gore as a company where people choose their managers. However their website makes clear that the people they are choosing are "sponsors (not bosses)". There are "no chains of command" and instead associates communicate directly with each other.

383. **Appointing the CEO:** Even the appointment of the new CEO is a group decision, with the opinions of dozens of staff members being sought.

Key Factors for a Happy Workplace

John went on to explain the key factors that he felt make W. L. Gore a happy workplace:

1. Clarity of commitment that's written by you.
2. Ability to use your strengths – so, you're in your sweet spot.
3. Rewards decided by your peers – so the team that you respect and you work for and you help deliver things, judges whether you've done a good job or not.
4. You work in teams that know and trust each other; hopefully you've got a good friend that's in there.

5. And most importantly, a voice that is heard. If you don't have a voice, what are you in the meeting for? Why don't you just read the meeting notes? If it's a communication of "this is what it's going to be" then just get the dictum afterwards. If you're in a meeting, I'm expecting a voice. I want to know your opinion.

Its guiding principles include Commitment ("We are not assigned tasks; rather, we each make our own commitments and keep them") and Waterline ("Everyone at Gore consults with other knowledgeable associates before taking actions that might be 'below the waterline', causing serious damage to the enterprise").

384. **Don't tell people what to do:** In Gore's "lattice organisation", anyone can talk to anyone, and no one tells another what to do. "If you tell anybody what to do here, they'll never work for you again," one associate told Gary Hamel.

385. **Gore's definition of leadership:** Gore has a disarmingly simple working definition of leadership: a capability to attract followers, for which no other qualifications are a substitute.

W. L. Gore is quite secretive, regarding its culture as a competitive advantage. I know of no book written about it. Articles include this[33] (2008) and this[34] (2019) from the *Financial Times* (both paywalled); this piece[35] in the *Wall Street Journal* from Gary Hamel; and this speech[36] from John Housego at the 2016 Happy Workplaces Conference.

9. Select Managers Who Are Good at Managing

Too often managers are chosen because of their core skills or length of service, rather than their potential for getting the most out of people. Make sure your people are supported by somebody who is good at doing that, and find other routes for those whose strengths lie elsewhere. Even better, allow people to choose their own managers.

Or step away from managers, and create self-managing organisations.

> "70% of the variance in team engagement is determined solely by the manager. It's the manager."
>
> *It's the Manager*, Jim Clifton, Jim Harter

386. **Less than a third of people have the potential to be great managers:** Gallup believes that only one in ten people have the right talents to be a great manager and another 20% can get there with the right coaching and development. They suggest you should forget the rest, in terms of management roles. Gallup believes that only 18% of current managers have the talent to do the role. See "State of the American Manager", Gallup.[37]

387. Stop telling people what to do: That's it. Instead coach them.

388. **Are you a multiplier of your people's talent?:** "Do you act as the expert, setting strategy, making key decisions and protecting your people? Those are diminishing behaviours. Or do you search out the talent in your people, create debate and step out of the way, to become a multiplier?" [Multipliers, Liz Wiseman]

> "Excellence is learning the names and school year of all 14 of your team members' kids."

Extreme Humanism, Tom Peters

389. **Be a multiplier:** After a session on multipliers in our Happy Workplace Leadership Programme, we got this feedback:

"Following on from the multipliers and diminishers session I really reflected on my own leadership style. I realised that due to Covid backlogs and being short-staffed, I had lost sight of the team and was only focused on trying to get the waiting lists down. This had led me on occasion to be a diminisher rather than a multiplier. I called a team meeting and asked team members what THEIR ideas were for increasing efficiency, improving staff morale and what THEY would like to achieve in their own careers.

"The answers amazed me. Some people wanted to undertake research projects and write scientific abstracts to present at conferences/get published. Others had ideas about how to re-structure a specialist echo clinic to reduce wasted slots. I listened and listened. And then I enabled.

"Even the ideas I didn't think would work. The abstracts got written and accepted for publication leading to a real sense of pride from those involved. The waiting list shortened for the specialist echo clinic. Team members were happier and I was happier. Win win!" Rebecca Dobson, cardiologist in the NHS

390. **Find the right people to be managers and increase revenues by 27%:** That is the verdict of Gallup's 2015 "State of the American Manager" report. The best managers, they argue, "are gifted with the ability to inspire employees, drive outcomes, overcome adversity, hold people accountable, build strong relationships and make tough decisions based on performance rather than politics".

391. **Step up as a temporary manager:** Dom Monkhouse explains that he would get people to step up while giving them a safety net: "I'd like to make you a manager, but it's a temporary position, and for now, there's no pay rise."

That way if they aren't up to the job, it is easy to step back and get them to do the role they were previously great at. [Mind Your F**king Business, Dom Monkhouse]

> "When Gallup asked thousands of managers how they became managers, the top two reasons they gave were: success in a prior non-management role and tenure."
>
> *It's the Manager*, Jim Clifton, Jim Harper

The role of the manager

The role of the manager is not to tell people what to do. Instead it is to step out of the way, give your people trust and coach them to be their best.

> "I see 99% of my job as getting out of the way. Help set the direction, give assurance and then get out of the way."
> Alison Sturgess-Durden, Director, Mayden

392. **Google give their managers lots of people to manage:** At some companies there is an upper limit to how many people report to one manager. Eric Schmidt (then Google CEO) made clear that Google suggests a minimum of seven and that at one point the Head of Engineering had 130 direct reports.

"With that many direct reports – most managers have a lot more than seven – there simply isn't time to micro-manage." [How Google Works, Eric Schmidt]

393. **Calm the fish:** To get great pictures, an underwater photographer must make sure they don't disturb the fish with their presence.

"As a manager you need to aim for the same thing. When you walk around, your presence makes no difference – people behave as they would when you are not there." Donna Reeves, ex-Director, Kingfisher plc

394. **Trust people to do the job:** "I gave my team more responsibility and trusted them to do their job, I don't step in and take over, I allow them to stumble and learn. I ask questions with the intention to listen and change my opinion."

The result: 97% staff retention, "voice of the customer" up from 7.5 to 8.7 approval ratings and a 45% increase in profits, the best results the region has seen. Allen Castro, ATS

395. **Let your people decide:** Encourage people to call meetings with managers when they want them, not the other way round.

396. **Business is about people not numbers:** "Throw away your reports and your KPIs," explains founder John Timpson of Timpson, "and get out and talk to the people in your company. Business success is all about the people and making them feel valued."

> "Here is my radical proposition: a business leader's job is to create great teams that do amazing work on time. That's it. That's the job of management."
>
> *Powerful*, Patty McCord

397. **The manager's role is to stay out of the way:** "Google is famously viewed as a bottom-up company, one that empowers even very young employees to drive decision-making. The managers' role is mostly to stay out of the way, sometimes to help, but never to interfere too much." [Radical Candour, Kim Scott]

398. **Adding too much value:** "Whenever a team would share some proposal or business plan with me, I would make sure to tell them how to improve it. Marshall Goldsmith, I later learned, calls this 'adding too much value'. For years, I kept trying to solve problems for them. In retrospect, this must have deeply demoralized them.

"Decisions did not have to be made by me all the time. It had taken many years for me to get there, but I was ready to let go of all my inclinations to be perfect. It was liberating, both for me and for the organisation." [The Heart of Business, Hubert Joly]

399. **Give the quiet ones a voice:** Jony Ive, Apple's chief design officer, once said at an Apple University class that a manager's

most important role is to "give the quiet ones a voice" [Radical Candour, Kim Scott]

> "Enable your people to use their full potential, not just 60% (or less) of it. It's not about you as a manager. It's about the team. If you trust the team, they will show up."
> Donna Reeves, ex-Director, Kingfisher plc

400. **No managers but there are leaders:** At Nearsoft, a Mexican outsourcing company, they have never had managers. "We don't have bosses but we do have leaders," explained Anabel Montiel. "They emerge organically and last as long as needed. People do take ownership of certain processes." So who holds people to account?

"The team. If somebody isn't performing, the team intervenes. There's a lot of peer pressure to do a good job. You are accountable to a lot of people. Having freedom doesn't mean you can do whatever you want. It means there is not one person following you and making sure you do what you have to do. Instead we have an awful lot of feedback processes."

401. **Talk less, listen more:** Multipliers talk 10% or less of the time at team meetings, diminishers are likely to talk 30% or more. [Multipliers, Liz Wiseman]

402. **Be prepared to say "I don't know":** For Adele Paterson of IHP, this gives the chance for somebody else to step up.

403. **Day on the shop floor:** "Spend a day in uniform (or equivalent). Regularly spend a day on the shop floor, working with front-line staff." Rachel Street, CEO, Heart of Kent Hospice

404. **It is about humility:** Before Reed Hastings founded Netflix he was an engineer working round the clock. Over the course of the week his coffee cups would stack up around his desk. At the end of the week somebody (he presumed the caretaker) cleaned them all.

One morning he arrived at four o'clock in the morning and found his CEO was washing up his mugs. When Reed asked him why, the CEO said, "You do so much for us, and this is the one thing I can do for you." "The fact that he was doing it humbly and not getting credit for it made his personal example so compelling that I admired him. I would follow him to the end of the earth." [CEO Excellence, Carolyn Dewar, Scott Keller, and Vikram Malhotra]

405. **CEO makes breakfast:** At Israeli biotech company Pluristem, CEO Yaky Yanay makes a nutritious breakfast for staff every morning. Yaky has run an Ironman (the ultimate in triathlons) and is keen to keep his staff healthy.

406. **Managers cause stress:** The Workforce Institute at UKG surveyed[38] 3,400 people across 10 countries and found that 69% of workers said that managers impacted their mental health.

The study also found that more than 80 percent of employees would rather have good mental health than a high-paying job. Two-thirds of employees would take a pay cut for a job that better supports their mental wellness.

> "The role of the director is to create a space where the actors and actresses can become more than they have ever been before, more than they've dreamed of being."
> Robert Altman in his Oscar acceptance speech, 2006, in *The Excellence Dividend*, Tom Peters

Listen

> "My education in leadership began in Washington when I was an assistant to Defense Secretary William Perry. He was universally loved and admired by heads of state ... and our own and allied troops. A lot of that was because of the way he listened. Each person who talked to him had his complete, undivided attention. Everyone blossomed in his presence, because he was so respectful, and I realized I wanted to affect people the same way."
>
> *Extreme Humanism*, Tom Peters

407. **Think like a three-year-old:** "Instead of thinking you know the answers, regain the curiosity of a three-year-old. Wonder why and wonder why not. Ask lots of questions." Cathy Busani, MD, Happy

408. **Listen and seek to understand:** "At Apple, as at Google, a boss's ability to achieve results had a lot more to do with listening and seeking to understand than it did with telling people what to do; more to do with debating than directing; more to do with pushing people to decide than with being the decider; more to do with persuading than with giving orders; more to do with learning than with knowing." [Radical Candour, Kim Scott]

The role is to coach

Imagine that you have a manager who genuinely cares about you and wants you to be the best you can be. A manager who builds your confidence, who challenges you but also provides support – even when you get stuff wrong. A manager who asks you questions, rather than tells, and helps you find your own solutions.

Might you actually look forward to seeing your manager?

> "Today's employees want a coach, not a boss. Moving your managers from boss to coach not only increases employee engagement and improves performance, but it's also essential to changing your culture."
> *It's the Manager*, Jim Clifton, Jim Harter

409. **The most important behaviour of managers is to be a good coach:** Google researched what were the most effective behaviours of managers, based on analysis of tens of thousands of performance reviews. The result was Project Oxygen, which came up with eight positive behaviours. The top three were:

1. Be a good coach
2. Empower your people, don't micro-manage
3. Show interest in your people

"Project Oxygen initially set out to prove that managers don't matter and ended up demonstrating that good managers were crucial." [Work Rules, Laszlo Bock]

410. **Managers are there to support at Timpson:** Founder John Timpson says, "Our managers are not allowed to tell anybody what to do. Their key role is to listen."

They are also expected to know their people. One test of managers

A manager's key role is to just listen and know more about their staff. They need to understand them as a person.

is whether they can name the children of the people they manage.

411. **Weekly one-to-ones at Innocent:** At smoothie company Innocent the coaching role is seen as so important that every member of staff is expected to have a weekly one-to-one session with their manager. Their office has been designed to have lots of small private rooms for those sessions.

412. **From telling people what to do to coaching at Haier:** When Haier took over General Electric Appliances, CEO Kevin Nolan found he had to reinvent his role. He started by delegating wherever possible, empowering others to make decisions. "I became more of a coach: someone you can talk to instead of someone who tells you what to do." [Start-Up Factory, Joost Minaar, Pim de Morree, Bran van der Lecq]

413. **No managers, just coaches at Buurtzorg:** "At Buurtzorg, there is no managerial ladder to climb; coaches are selected for their coaching capacity – they tend to be older, highly experienced nurses with strong interpersonal skills. The span of support (what in traditional organisations would be called 'span of control') of Buurtzorg's regional coaches is broad; on average, a coach supports 40 to 50 teams.

"Coaches shouldn't have too much time on their hands, or they risk getting too involved with teams, and that would hurt teams' autonomy. Now they take care of only the most important questions. We gave some of the first teams from Buurtzorg quite intensive support and attention, and today we still see that they are more dependent and less autonomous than other teams." Jos de Blok, founder of Buurtzorg

414. **Coaches not managers:** I asked Jos why there were so few coaches for so many employees. His response: "so they don't start acting like managers".

> "I still get to do the 'people' stuff I loved as a manager, it's just that now I use a whole range of different techniques to support colleagues to find

their own solutions, and run with their own ideas. It's liberating."

    Alison Sturgess-Durdon, Director, Mayden

Let people choose their managers

For many people it is their manager who makes them unhappy at work. A CMI (Chartered Marketing Institute) survey found that 49% would take a pay cut if they were able to change their manager.

So why don't we let people choose a different manager? It may not make sense in a traditional hierarchical organisation. However in a more flexible workplace, especially where the role of the manager is to coach, why would you not let people choose their managers?

415. **Choose your manager at W. L. Gore:** At Gore, makers of Goretex, you can choose anybody to play that role. The person you choose is your champion.

416. **Over 20 years of choosing your manager at Happy:** At Happy people have been able to choose their manager since 2000. As we have moved towards becoming a self-managing organisation, this choice has switched to choosing your coach.

417. **Choose your counsellor at EY:** At most management consultancies employees are engaged on projects for months or years. Yet the person who manages the project is rarely their actual manager.

At EY they have a counsellor. "The role is to create a degree of consistency, take care of their career, their development, the pastoral aspect," explains Amanda Gethin, Head of HR.

One friend at EY told me they were on the verge of leaving at the end of their first year, because they didn't get on with their counsellor. Then a colleague told them they could change their counsellor. They did so and have gone on to thrive.

418. **Choosing managers in the public sector:** At one public sector organisation in the West Country a department of 600 people lets people choose their manager. There is a spreadsheet,

where each manager spells out how many people they would like to manage and what they feel they can contribute.

One individual told me that they had chosen three different managers over five years, not because they had difficulties but because they saw different needs. "I now feel like I am in charge of my career progression."

419. **Choose your team at DreamHost:** The Los Angeles-based web hosting provider followed a practice of "choose your favourite product to work on", and let people choose their own team, rather than being allocated one. They say this resulted in greater efficiency and increased performance from giving team members a choice. [Worldblu, 50 transformational practices]

420. **Choose another team at any time:** "At FAVI, a simple but powerful relief valve exists, should a team leader find the taste of power too sweet: workers can choose at any moment to join another team." [Reinventing Organisations, Frederick Laloux]

> "Your title makes you a manager. Your people make you a leader."
>
> Debbie Biondolillo, Apple's former Head of Human Resources, in *How Google Works*, Eric Schmidt

Two tracks of promotion

> "The best organizations believe that not everyone should be a manager, and they create high-value career paths for individual contributor roles. No one should feel like their progress depends on getting promoted to manager."
>
> *It's the Manager*, Jim Clifton, Jim Harper

When I suggest that people should choose their manager, I am often asked "what about the people that don't get chosen?" My answer is that they are often delighted, as people management is not always for them.

One employee told me how, when they started their new job, their manager came up to them and said, "I'm not really a people person. I probably won't remember your name. I'd much rather be sitting at my desk writing reports." That manager should be at their desk writing reports (and being paid well if they are good at it), but should never be in charge of people.

For this you need two tracks of management, one for those who want to manage people and one for those who are good at their core skill.

421. **Create "Dual Career Tracks":** Hay Group explains DCTs: "The defining attribute of a dual career track is that, at some point in the path, the individual is presented with a choice." Employees get to choose between a managerial career, or one of expertise which does not involve people responsibilities. Although the concept of DCTs has existed for decades, this practice has mostly been used by a handful of world-leading technology and science companies.

422. **Cougar created a judo belt system for reward:** Happy was training engineers from software company Cougar in management skills. At the end of the day, several managers approached the facilitator and said "This isn't really for us. We're going to approach our MD and ask if we can stop being managers."

Clive Hutchinson, Cougar's Managing Director, turned out to be open to this. The company created a second career path for those who wanted to remain engineers, based around the judo belt system. Engineers would start as a light blue belt, and move up through white and brown to the ultimate black belt. It has proved highly successful as an alternative career path.

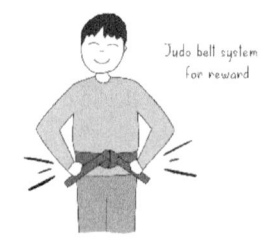

Judo belt system for reward

Career paths can be designed in many ways. Not everyone wants to become a Manager!

423. **Not everybody wants to be a manager:** Apple was founded by Steve Jobs and Steve Wozniak, known as Woz. For Mike Markulla, the initial investor, a condition of that investment was that both Steves were on board as full-time employees of Apple.

So Steve Jobs went to Woz and explained that he would no longer be a small cog, but would manage a whole team of engineers. Woz said no, he reckoned he'd stay at HP. Jobs kept trying to persuade him, emphasising his importance and how many people he'd be in charge of.

But Mike Markulla actually understood something that Jobs did not. He took Steve Jobs aside and explained that Woz just wanted to be an engineer. He didn't want to be responsible for other people.

Jobs changed his approach: he offered Woz great kit, all the resources he needed and promised "Woz, you will never have to manage anybody." That sounded good to Woz and he made the move. The rest is history.

424. **Mastercard have special career paths for people who want to progress but not manage people:** Employees can either progress as consultants (functional) or leaders (managerial). They have these paths in project management and sales, and plan to implement them in product development, marketing and

communications. Mastercard has often been in the top 50 best companies to work for.

425. **The Post-it note would not exist without dual tracks:** One of the most tangible results of a dual career track system is the existence of the Post-it. Arthur Fry at 3M was responsible for developing the best-selling product. According to Fry, the Post-it would not have existed today if 3M's dual career paths had not been in place. Fry admitted that one of the reasons behind his choice to remain in the field, and not pursue a managerial career, was because of the possibility of becoming one of their highly regarded "corporate scientists".[39] [Rethinking the Corporation: The Architecture of Change, Robert Tomasko].

426. **Triple career tracks at BP:** Another company that has reported the success of their multiple careers system is BP. They have a triple career system: functional specialists, functional leaders and business leaders. They do however encourage moving between the categories.

427. **Triple tracks again at Rolls-Royce:** At Rolls-Royce, they pursue a similar approach to that of BP. There are three types of manager: specialist roles (functional), technical manager (functional) and project manager (traditional). Rolls-Royce have received praise for their internal structures and have often been in the top 25 best companies to work for in the UK.

428. **The individual contributor at Google:** Google's engineering teams solved this problem by creating an "individual contributor" career path that is more prestigious than the manager path and sidesteps management entirely. This has been great for the growth of engineers and is also good for the people whom they would otherwise have been managing. When people become bosses just to "get ahead" rather than because they want to do what bosses do, they perform, at best, a perfunctory job and often become bosses from hell. [Radical Candour, Kim Scott]

Elect your leaders

> "If your actions inspire others to dream more, learn more, do more and become more, you are a leader."
>
> John Quincy Adams

429. **Rotating leadership at Orpheus Chamber Orchestra:** At this Grammy award-winning orchestra there is no conductor, and leadership roles are rotated amongst orchestra members, establishing fairness and dignity for all the musicians. [Worldblu, 50 transformational practices]

430. **All staff evaluate the CEO:** At the DaVita medical group, all of the 74,500 employees are asked to rate the CEO, Kent Thiry, on how well he is living DaVita's seven core values. His scores are presented on stage in front of 3,000 managers at their annual national conference. [WorldBlu, 50 Transformation Practices]

431. **Elect your leaders at AIESEC:** At the "world's largest youth-run organisation", present in more than 180 countries, the international leadership team is elected every year – and has been for over 60 years. [Worldblu, 50 transformational practices]

Case Study: Basecamp

Basecamp is a software company, producing the project management tool called, you guessed it, Basecamp. However it doesn't act like most software companies, or indeed like most companies. The following quotes are taken from the book *It Doesn't Have to be Crazy at Work* by Jason Fried and David Heinemeier Hansson.

432. **Put life ahead of work:** Instead of offering benefits to keep people in the office, like free food and laundry, they offer "not a single benefit that would make someone prefer to be at work rather than at home. Not a single benefit that puts work ahead of life." One example is that they pay for the cost of their employees' holidays.

433. **No long hours:** Instead of encouraging long hours, they discourage them: "Working 40 hours a week is plenty. Plenty of time to do great work, plenty of time to be competitive, plenty of time to get the important stuff done. So that's how long we work at Basecamp. No more. Less is often fine, too. During the summer (which, for Basecamp, is five months, from May to September) we even take Fridays off and still get plenty of good stuff done in just 32 hours."

434. **Stay small**: Instead of aiming to grow, they aim to "stay as small as we can for as long as we can".

Doing nothing is an option

435. **Pare it down:** "Doing nothing isn't an option" is a common business phrase. Basecamp's response: "Oh, yes, it is. And it's often the best one. Rather than

Cutting down and lightening the load can lead to a more profitable company

continue to invent new products, take on more responsibilities, and grow more obligations, we continually aim to pare down and lighten the load – even when times are great. Cutting back when times are great is the luxury of a calm, profitable, and independent company."

436. **Stop with the ideas:** As leaders they try to hold back: "It takes great restraint as the leader of an organization not to keep lobbing ideas at everyone else. Every such idea is a pebble that's going to cause ripples when it hits the surface. Throw enough pebbles in the pond and the overall picture becomes as clear as mud."

> "If you can't fit everything you want to do within 40 hours per week, you need to get better at picking what to do, not work longer hours. Most of what we think we have to do, we don't have to do at all. It's a choice, and often it's a poor one."

Effectiveness not busyness

437. **Be effective not busy:** "We don't believe in busyness at Basecamp. We believe in effectiveness. How little can we do? How much can we cut out? Instead of adding to-dos, we add to-don'ts … The only way to get more done is to have less to do."

New ideas are rarely implemented immediately. Instead of "jumping on every new idea right away, we make every idea wait a while. Generally a few weeks, at least."

438. **Not everything has to be great:** Rather than putting endless effort into every detail, they put lots of effort into separating what really matters, from what sort of matters, from what doesn't matter at all: "The act of separation should be your highest quality endeavour. It's easy to say, 'Everything has to be great', but anyone can do that. The challenge lies in figuring out where you can be just kinda okay or even downright weak."

439. **Office hours:** Basecamp tries to create an atmosphere where it's easy to get stuff done. Instead of encouraging people to be available at all times, they publish "office hours", the times when subject matter experts are available.

"Taking someone's time should be a pain in the ass. Taking many people's time should be so cumbersome that most people won't even bother to try it unless it's REALLY IMPORTANT! Meetings should be a last resort, especially big ones."

440. **JOMO:** "Most people should miss out on most things most of the time. That's what we try to encourage at Basecamp. JOMO! The joy of missing out."

441. **Keep teams small:** They aim not to throw more people at problems. Instead "we chop problems down until they can be carried across the finish line by teams of three."

> "Any conversation with more than three people is typically a conversation with too many people."

442. **At Basecamp the front-line staff make the key decisions:** "And who makes the decision about what stays and what goes in a fixed period of time? The team that's working on it. Not the CEO, not the CTO. The team that's doing the work has control over the work. They wield the 'scope hammer', as we call it."

> "Choose calm."

As the magazine *Inc* puts it:[40] "Instead of managers, the company looks for people who can direct their own work and actually produce something, rather than watch others produce."

10. Play to Your Strengths

Dan Pink, author of *Drive* and many other management books, talks about motivation being down to mastery, autonomy and purpose. Mastery is about doing what you are good at, playing to your strengths.

443. **Focus on strengths and double your engagement:** Gallup has found clear correlations between a managerial focus on employees' strengths (as compared to strengths and weaknesses or only weaknesses) and employee engagement: 67% of the respondents who said that their manager used a strengths-based approach were engaged at work, compared to 30% overall. See State of the American Manager,[41] Gallup.

> "Only 21% of employees strongly agree that their organization is committed to building the strengths of each employee."
> *It's the Manager*, Jim Clifton, Jim Harper

444. **Delegate to teams, not individuals:** Often managers have one or more go-to people that they like to delegate to. At Happy we decided to stop delegating to individuals. Instead we delegate to the team and they decide who is best placed to do a task, whose strength it plays to.

445. **Enable people to play to their strengths:** At Happy, Cathy Busani (MD) explained, all staff have used Strengthfinder to understand their strengths. "I facilitate sessions where we look at everybody's jobs and people choose to change what they do to better fit what they like doing and what they are good at."

At Happy everybody's 5 key strengths are on the organisational chart.

(Strengthfinder establishes your five key strengths. You can get a code to the online questionnaire in Now Discover Your Strengths by Marcus Buckingham or StrengthFinder 2.0 by Don Clifton.)

Find joy in 80% of your work: The aim at Happy is for all staff to find joy in at least 80% of their work. Generally, this means people working to their strengths and doing what they are good at. If it doesn't give them joy, everyone is encouraged to find a different way of doing it or find somebody in the team for whom it does give joy. Everybody estimates their level of joy in the quarterly snapshots. The latest snapshots give an average of 87%, for how much joy people find in their work.

> "Start with what gives you energy and joy – in short, what drives you?"
> *The Heart of Business*, Hubert Joly

446. **Build a team where each person does what they are good at:** Neuroscientist and academic Stephen Kosslyn once gave a talk in which he described how people who work together on a team become like "mental prostheses" for each other. What one person doesn't enjoy and isn't good at is what another person loves and excels at. Together, they are "better, stronger, faster" [Radical Candour, Kim Scott]

447. **Find your strengths:** "What, last week, did you look forward to, helped you stay inquisitive, and left you feeling magnificent? That is where to find your strengths." Marcus Buckingham

448. **Throw away the job descriptions:** Instead of sticking to job descriptions, try throwing the job roles in the air. Get each team member to put each of their roles on a Post-it on the wall. Then get people to decide which they want to do in the next period. Ask what people love doing, and they are good at.

449. **Focus on what you do best:** Dom Monkhouse describes how one of his clients employs a "phenomenal salesperson", but they are hopeless at administrative tasks such as booking meetings and completing the CRM (Customer Relationship Management). So the client hired a personal assistant to do that stuff for him. "He no longer does any admin tasks himself. He

focuses solely on what he does best." [Mind Your F**king Business, Dom Monkhouse]

450. **Get rid of individual job descriptions:** "We moved from individual job descriptions to team descriptions. We agree what the team needs to do and then let the individuals figure out who does what." Cathy Busani, MD, Happy

Case Study: Netflix

This chapter is based on the book *No Rules Rules: Netflix and the Culture of Reinvention* by Reed Hastings and Erin Meyer.

A culture of freedom and responsibility

451. **Trust your people:** The Netflix culture has a remarkable level of trust. When Sheryl Sandberg, Chief Operating Officer at Facebook, spent a day shadowing Reed Hastings she commented: "The amazing thing was to sit with you all day long and see that you didn't make one decision!"

452. **Lead with context, not control:** Netflix is not of course a self-managing organisation. Instead of telling people what to do, though, managers are expected to set the context.

Adam Del Deo, head of Netflix's documentaries, was wondering whether to increase his $2.5 million bid for the documentary *Icarus*. He asked his boss, Ted Sarandos, if he should bid more.

Ted responded not with a decision but with context: "Is it THE ONE? Is it going to be a massive hit? If it's THE ONE, get the movie."

As Reed continues, "When one of your people does something dumb, don't blame that person. Instead, ask yourself what context you failed to set."

453. **Farm for dissent:** But Netflix staff are not expected to make decisions on their own. Instead the approach is similar to the Advice Process: "We don't expect employees to get approval from their boss before they make decisions. But we do know that good decisions require a solid grasp of the context, feedback from people with different perspectives, and awareness of all the options."

If someone uses the freedom Netflix gives them to make important decisions without soliciting others' viewpoints, Netflix considers that a demonstration of poor judgement.

If you are a Netflix employee with a proposal, you create a shared memo explaining the idea and inviting dozens of your colleagues for input. They will then leave comments electronically in the margin of your document, which everyone can view.

"Farm for dissent. Socialize the idea. Test it out. This sounds a lot like consensus building, but it's not. With consensus building the group decides; at Netflix a person will reach out to relevant colleagues, but does not need to get anyone's agreement before moving forward. They are the Informed Captain."

454. **Mistakes?:** While you may be fired if you are felt to be performing only adequately, you won't get fired for getting something wrong. "At Netflix, we try to shine a bright light on every failed bet. We encourage employees to write open memos explaining candidly what happened, followed by a description of the lessons learned."

455. **Don't seek to please your boss, seek to do what is best for the company:** "At most companies, even at those who have leaders who don't micro-manage, employees seek to make the decision the boss is most likely to support," explains Reed.

456. **It is disloyal not to express your opinion:** There are lots of examples in the book of where Netflix staff do the opposite of what the boss would support. In one case senior director Ted Sarandos is discussing the release of *The Blacklist* season 2, and a guy four levels down hierarchically from Ted "pipes up and tells him he was missing something and hadn't understood the licence deal". At the end of the session Ted thanks him for his contribution.

"We now say that it is disloyal to Netflix when you disagree with an idea and do not express that disagreement. By withholding your opinion, you are implicitly choosing to not help the company."

No Rules Rules

457. **Unlimited holidays:** Netflix is famous for its vacation policy ("take some") and its expenses policy ("act in Netflix's best interest").

On the need for holidays, Reed gives the example of a guy who "often went to an isolated place. Each time he came back he had a fantastic new idea for how to move the business forward." However, unlimited holidays depend crucially on the example from managers. While Reed takes six weeks off a year, Erin makes it clear that some managers take less. In turn their staff feel unable to take advantage of the policy.

458. **Act in Netflix's best interests:** Interestingly the expenses policy was originally "spend money as if it were your own" but this didn't work for those who were profligate spenders in their personal life. Reed reckons the expenses policy probably results in 10% extra spending (due to business class travel on airlines) but is well worth it in terms of trust and speed: "Approval policies, decision-making by committee, and contract sign-offs all put hurdles in front of your employees so that they can't move quickly."

This is in contrast to his previous company, Push Software. There they had all sorts of policies: "we had, without much thought, dummy-proofed the work environment. The result was that only dummies wanted to work there."

Pump up Candour

459. **Help your colleagues improve:** Netflix takes feedback seriously, at every level. Staff are expected to provide others with clear candour to help them improve.

Indeed it is so embedded that Erin Meyer describes how, as an outside speaker, she received clear feedback in the middle of her talk. Giving a presentation on international cultural differences, she was told she was undermining her message, as she always went to the first people to raise their hands for questions – who were normally Americans. As a result she was able to change her approach for the rest of the talk.

460. **Stop, Start, Continue:** Initially there was an annual survey based on "Stop, Start, Continue" (what should this person stop doing, start doing, continue doing). However now the most common approach is to hire a private room in a restaurant for a team and, over the meal, get everybody to provide feedback to each of their colleagues.

A core principle here is: "Only say about someone what you will say to their face."

It sounds impressive. We all know we would like to improve but few companies provide true radical candour.

Erin reveals the figures from a survey: "57 percent of respondents claim they would prefer to receive corrective feedback to positive feedback. 72 percent felt their performance would improve if they received more corrective feedback. 92 percent agreed with the comment, 'Negative feedback, if delivered appropriately, improves performance'."

Stop, Start, Continue
Only say about someone what you would say to their face

461. **Stop being busy**: Among all this I love the fact that Reed is not one of those executives who works all hours and is endlessly busy. In February 2020, just before the pandemic, I wrote a LinkedIn post[42] stating that, as a CEO, I was not busy. I argued that senior people "need to step out of the way, stop with the endless meetings and get a life."

However, I am head of a 25-person company. Reed Hastings runs a $25 billion enterprise, employing 10,000 people. So I am delighted

170

to find he agrees: Reed "believes so deeply in dispersed decision-making that, by his model, only a CEO who is not busy is really doing his job".

The results have been astounding. $10,000 invested in Netflix at its public offering in 2002 would be worth $3.5 million now. Netflix currently has a higher revenue per employee even than Apple. And, according to a 2018 survey from Hired, Netflix rated no. 1 (above Apple and Google) as the place tech workers would most like to work for.

The Challenge

While Netflix has a huge level of trust and freedom, it does also have some potentially controversial elements:

462. **Adequate performance gets a generous severance package:** That is the controversial proposal that was originally shared in the Netflix Culture Deck. As Erin points out, this appears to violate the principles of "psychological safety", that if you want to encourage innovation you should develop an environment "where people feel safe to dream, to speak up and take risks".

Reed explains that this approach results from 2001, when Netflix had to make redundancies and kept those they saw as most talented: "we'd just let go of a third of the workforce, yet the office was suddenly buzzing with passion, energy, and ideas. Suddenly, we were doing far more work – with 30 percent fewer employees … We learned that a company with really dense talent is a company everyone wants to work for."

463. **The keeper test:** Every manager at Netflix is encouraged to consider, for each of their people: "If a person on your team were to quit tomorrow, would you try to change their mind?"

If the answer is no, then it's time to let them go. There is no four-month PIP (Performance Improvement Plan). They are paid off straight away with an adequate severance package.

Why is this in a book on happy workplaces? Two reasons: one is that people prefer to work with strong performers. And sometimes the job isn't the right one for you.

> *"Everybody is good at something"*
> **Michael Young**

11. Self-Managing Organisations

"How many of you have managers?" asked Alison Sturgess-Durden at the 2019 Happy Workplaces Conference. Lots of hands were raised. "How many of you feel you need to be managed?" she continued. Nobody raised their hand.

Alison, a director at the software company Mayden, asked why we assume that people need to be "managed" at work, when they don't need to be managed at home. Mayden is one of a growing band of companies that have no managers.

This is one of the big developments since the publication of *The Happy Manifesto*. There were some self-managing companies at the time. Gary Hamel had just written his article for *Harvard Business Review*, entitled "First, let's fire all the managers", based on the US tomato processing company Morning Star.

Companies like W. L. Gore and Semco also had elements of self-management. However the idea really came to prominence when Frederick Laloux published *Reinventing Organisations* in 2016. This used the term "Teal" to describe the future of organisations, based on self-managing. He included a dozen such companies.

Red represents where power is held by a dominant individual. Amber where there are hierarchies and rules. Green is about collaboration, empowerment and employee well-being. Teal represents the "evolutionary" stage where organisations operate as self-managing, decentralised entities with a strong sense of purpose and adaptability.

Buurtzorg, Reddico, Haier and W. L. Gore have been covered earlier. Here are some more examples of organisations that have no managers.

464. **Morning Star:** Morning Star, a $700 million tomato processing company, has had no managers since its foundation in

1970. "By making the mission the boss and truly empowering people, the company creates an environment where people can manage themselves." Here's the classic HBR piece[43] by Gary Hamel in 2011.

In "First, let's fire all the managers", Gary Hamel argued that "A hierarchy of managers exacts a hefty tax on any organisation." A centrally planned approach works no better within an organisation than it did in the Eastern European economies, and is a huge waste of time, money and resources.

465. **Mayden**: Mayden, based in Bath in the UK, switched to a flat structure[44] where "everyone would have an equal say in the life and direction of the company." Instead of managers there are "volunteer internal peer coaches" who support their colleagues and help them find their own solutions.

466. **u2i:** u2i is a web technology consulting company based in Krakow in Poland (though with a Head Office in New York). Employing around 60 people, it is renowned for being largely self-managing and for the fact that it distributes fully 100% of its profits in bonuses to employees. Instead of managers they have "Sherpas" to coach and guide. More here.[45]

467. **Zappos:** US online shoe delivery company Zappos has long been an inspiration. Founder Tony Hsieh outlined his belief in creating a happy working environment in his best-seller *Delivering Happiness*. In 2014 they adopted the Holacracy idea of "management without managers" (Holacracy is a system where authority is distributed across self-managing teams rather than being concentrated in a hierarchical structure.)

468. **Valve:** Valve is a 400-strong games software company, whose value has been estimated at over $1 billion. It has been manager-free since it was founded in 1996. Check out its brilliant Employee Handbook.[46] Of Managing Director Gabe Newall, it says "of all the people in the company who are not your boss, Gabe is the MOST not your boss." It also includes a remarkably honest "What Valve is not good at" section.

The freedom to not have a boss can lead to amazing things

As its website says: "When you give smart talented people the freedom to create without fear of failure, amazing things happen." Unusually it puts its approach[47] down to the political theory of anarcho-syndicalism.

Valve accomplishes all this with a highly unconventional approach to authority. It simply lets its employees decide what to work on. No bosses. No reporting. No oversight. Just "vote with your feet" by choosing projects and tasks that you think are worth your time.

469. **GitHub:** A coding company with around 40 employees. One explains:[48] "We do things differently at GitHub: we work out of chat rooms, we don't enforce hours, and we have zero managers. People work on what they want to work on. Product development is driven by whoever wants to drive product."

470. **Medium:** Jason Stirman explains[49] how he discovered as a manager at Twitter that asking "What's going on in your life?" was far more effective than asking "What's blocking you at work?" At Medium, they have adopted Holacracy.

471. **North West Care Cooperative (UK):** A small, emerging, CQC-registered co-operative provider of care, or as they prefer to think of it, a "community" whose "users", "employees" (à la

Buurtzorg) and "supporting" members care about each other. Learn more on their Twitter, @NWCareCoop.

472. **Cocoon:** an Italian-based bedding company, though now present across four countries, Cocoon uses an open governance framework that they have called a Liquid Organisation. Read all about it here.[50]

473. **Happy:** At Happy we don't have managers either. We have what we call M&Ms (Mentors and Multipliers), though they could also be described as coaches. They help and support our people to work out how to work at their best. This may be old-fashioned compared to some of the companies above, but we do believe our people benefit from having somebody to guide and support them.

So think about it. Do your managers enhance your work and enable your people? If so, great! Or do they take up huge amount of time and resources doing that management thing?

Remember the CMI survey[51] that found that 49% so dislike their manager that they would take a pay cut to be managed by somebody else.

There is another way. Perhaps it's time for more organisations to try doing away with managers?

12. The Evidence for Happy Workplaces

There is a growing body of research that shows that creating a working environment where people feel happy and fulfilled is one of the most effective ways to create organisations that are more productive in every way.

The evidence shows that they are more productive, more profitable, have lower costs, less staff turnover and stronger share growth.

Some of the research below is based explicitly on how happy people are. Some is based on employee engagement, or great workplace lists. However all of it is based on organisations that have made creating a great workplace culture a priority.

474. **Research shows that what enables productivity is empowering people:** Dr Kamal Birdi of the University of Sheffield and six other researchers studied the productivity of 308 companies across 22 years. They found that approaches like "total quality management" and "just-in-time inventory control" had no consistent effect on productivity.

This research is quoted by Laszlo Bock (Head of People at Google) in his book *Work Rules*. So what did work? "Performance improved only when companies implemented programs to empower employees (for example, by taking decision-making authority away from managers and giving it to individuals or teams), provided learning opportunities that were outside what people needed to do their jobs, increased their reliance on teamwork (by giving teams more autonomy and allowing them to self-organize), or a combination of these."

475. **The benefit of engaged staff:** "When Gallup analysed the differences in performance between engaged and actively disengaged business/work units, work units scoring in the top quartile on employee engagement significantly outperformed

those in the bottom quartile on these crucial performance outcomes:

- 41% lower absenteeism
- 24% less staff turnover (in high-turnover organisations)
- 59% less staff turnover (in low-turnover organisations)
- 70% fewer safety incidents
- 40% fewer defects (quality)
- 10% higher customer ratings
- 17% higher productivity
- 20% higher sales
- 21% higher profitability"

[It's the Manager, Jim Clifton, Jim Harper, Gallup]

Happy workplaces are more profitable

476. **Engaged workers deliver better results:** "Business units with engaged workers have 23% higher profit compared with business units with miserable workers. Additionally, teams with thriving workers see significantly lower absenteeism, turnover and accidents; they also see higher customer loyalty. The point is: Wellbeing at work isn't at odds with anyone's agenda." Jon Clifton, CEO, Gallup in their 2022 *Global Workplace Report*.

477. **Happy employees lead to greater revenue growth:** In Harvard psychologist Daniel Goleman's book *Primal Leadership*, one study shows that for every 2% increase in how happy employees are, revenue grew by 1%.

478. **Employee engagement leads to stronger margins:** A three-year study of 41 global companies found "operating margins improved nearly 4% on average in organizations with high employee engagement levels and declined about 2% in those with low engagement levels." They concluded that there is a "clear relationship between high levels of employee engagement and improved financial and operational results". See "The Power of Three: Taking Engagement to New Heights",[52] Willis Tower Watson, May 2019.

479. **The danger of disengaged workers:** In contrast one study[53] found that where employees are disengaged, they cost businesses in the US somewhere between $450 and $550 billion a year. [DNA of Engagement: How Organizations Can Foster Employee Ownership of Engagement. The Engagement Institute]

Happy workplaces have lower costs

480. **Engaged employees have lower sickness rates:** In Germany, Gallup found that days of sickness for engaged and thriving employees averaged 3.9 days a year versus 10.7 for actively disengaged and suffering employees. See "Low Employee Well-Being and Engagement Hurt German Companies",[54] Marco Nink, *Gallup Business Journal*, April 2013.

	Engaged	Not Engaged	Actively Disengaged
Thriving	3.9	4.9	6.5
Struggling	5.3	6.6	7.7
Suffering	*	7.5	10.7

NOTE: Sick days missed per year.   * insufficient sample size

GALLUP

In the US, 550 million days a year are lost due to workplace stress.

481. **Highly engaged workplaces have 41% less sickness and 59% less staff turnover:** In its 2017 US "State of the American Workplace" report, Gallup found dramatic differences between the top quartile most-engaged workplaces and the bottom quartile. See "State of the American Workplace",[55] Gallup, 2017.

WHEN COMPARED WITH BUSINESS UNITS IN THE BOTTOM QUARTILE OF ENGAGEMENT, THOSE IN THE TOP QUARTILE REALIZE **IMPROVEMENTS** IN THE FOLLOWING AREAS:

Absenteeism	Turnover (High-Turnover Organizations)	Turnover (Low-Turnover Organizations)	Shrinkage
41% LOWER	24% LOWER	59% LOWER	28% LESS

Safety Incidents	Patient Safety Incidents	Quality Defects (Defects)	Customer Metrics
70% FEWER	58% FEWER	40% FEWER	10% HIGHER

Productivity	Sales	Profitability
17% HIGHER	20% HIGHER	21% HIGHER

GALLUP

482. **Employees with higher job satisfaction are less likely to leave:** Not surprising, perhaps. A Columbia University study found that job satisfaction is less likely to lead to people leaving the company. See "Job Satisfaction and Employee Turnover Intention: What does Organizational Culture Have To Do With It?",[56] Elizabeth Medina, Columbia Academic Commons.

Happy workplaces, more share growth

There have been a large number of studies showing that great places to work produce better stock market returns.

483. **Investing in the Fortune best workplaces produced a 136% greater growth than the S&P share index:** Analysis of a value-weighted portfolio of the Fortune "100 best companies to work for in America" resulted in an average of 3.5% greater return per year from 1984 to 2009. This means that compared to an investment in the S&P that ended up with $100,000 in 2009, investing in the best workplaces (changing the portfolio each year) would have produced $236,000. See "Does the stock market fully value intangibles?",[57] Alex Edmans, Wharton Business School, 2010.

484. **Over 17 years, the best places to work grew at over three times the rate of the standard stock market:** Stock market listed companies in the Fortune "100 best companies to work for" in 1997 grew by 495% in the 17 years to 2013, compared to 170% for the Russell 3000 and 156% for the S&P 500. See "Treat Employees Well, See Stock Price Soar",[58] David McCann, cfo.com, 2014.

485. **Glassdoor "best places to work" companies increased their share value by twice the level of the stock market:** Investing in stock market listed companies in the Glassdoor "100 best places to work" companies from 2009 to 2019 resulted in a 553% stock market growth compared to 258% for the standard S&P. See "How Do Satisfied Employees Impact Stock Performance?",[59] Dr Andrew Chamberlain and Zanele Munyikwa, *Glassdoor Economic Research Blog*, 2020.

486. **Great workplaces have earnings per share growth that is 4.3 times greater than competitors:** Gallup studied the performance of its Great Workplace award winners and found 115% growth in EPS (Earnings Per Share), compared to 27% for competitors. See "State of the American Workplace Report",[60] Gallup, 2017.

Happy workplaces in the public sector

487. **Fewer patients die if hospital staff are happy and engaged:** The Kings Fund found[61] that for every 96 patients who die in a hospital with highly engaged staff, 103 die where staff have low engagement. That means over 5,000 deaths a year, in the UK alone, result from poor organisational culture. Or, as I prefer to say, 5,000 lives are saved by happy, engaged hospitals.

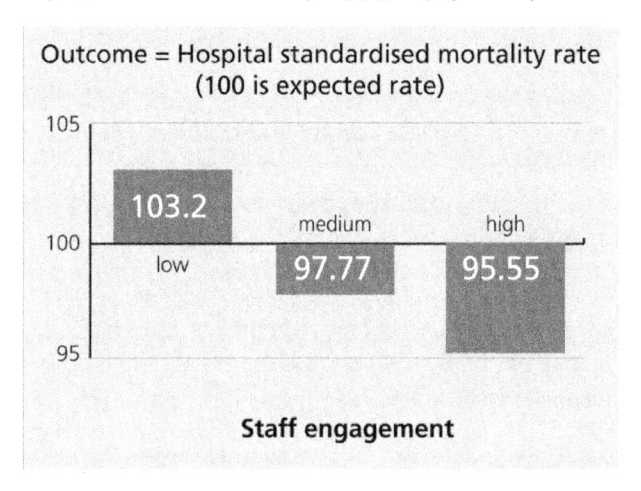

Outcome = Hospital standardised mortality rate (100 is expected rate)

Staff engagement	Rate
low	103.2
medium	97.77
high	95.55

488. **More control over your work makes you healthier:** The Whitehall Study,[62] which is the largest longitudinal study of people in the workplace ever conducted, found connections between better wellbeing and positive outcomes, and also direct causes. It has investigated more than 10,000 UK civil servants since 1985 and a key finding was that how much control you have, and how much opportunity there is for social participation, profoundly affects the health of individuals. The conclusion was that there is an intrinsic need for autonomy and social engagement.

More benefits of happy workplaces

489. **Greater customer loyalty and higher productivity:** Christian Krekel, George Ward and Jan-Emmanuel de Neve from Said Business School explored Gallup studies[63] involving 1.9 million employees across 230 organisations in 73 countries.

They found employee satisfaction had a substantial positive correlation with customer loyalty and higher productivity, a negative link with staff turnover and – less strongly – with profitability.

490. **Happy workers are less likely to leave:** Brooks Holton of Georgetown University found that[64] if workers are more connected to their jobs, their co-workers and the firm, they are less likely to leave.

491. **Focus on meaning:** A University of Alberta study[65] showed that companies who help staff to focus on the purpose and meaning in their positions showed a 60% drop in absenteeism and a 75% reduction in staff turnover.

492. **Engage your employees for a competitive advantage:** A Hay Group Study[66] reported that 94% of the world's most admired companies believe that their efforts to engage their employees have created a competitive advantage. 85% of these companies believed that their efforts to engage employees had reduced employee performance problems.

493. **Be happy and be more productive:** The well-cited study[67] from Warwick University in 2012 managed to quantify the relationship between happy employees and productivity: half of the participants were exposed to mood-enhancing factors such as comedy clips before trying to solve problems and puzzles, while the other half embarked on the problems directly without being exposed to the clips. The first test group solved the problems much faster, and were 12% more productive.

494. **Happy workers are 31% more productive and generate 37% more sales:** And they are three times more creative. This is taken from Shawn Achor's article "'Positive Intelligence"[68] in the *Harvard Business Review*. It is based on research by Sonia Lyubomirsky, Laura King and Ed Diener: "The Benefits of Frequent Positive Affect: Does Happiness Lead to Success?"[69]

495. **Focus on employee wellbeing:** Clinical psychologist and business consultant Dr Noelle Nelson has written the book *Make More Money by Making Your Employees Happy*. Her research shows that companies who realise the value in focusing on employee wellbeing and take actions to promote it have three times higher ROE (Return on Equity) than firms that do not.

Dr Nelson gives a good example[70] of this in practice: when Paul O'Neill became CEO of manufacturing firm Alcoa in 1987, he shocked the Board members by announcing that his primary priority was to improve worker safety. O'Neill had realised this was a major issue for the staff. In the following 13 years, accident rates dropped massively while productivity soared. By the time O'Neill stepped down, Alcoa's annual revenues had increased by 500%.

496. **Customer retention rates are higher when staff are engaged:** Software provider Cvent found in a 2014 study[71] that customer retention rates are on average 18% higher when employees are actively engaged at work.

Happy people live longer and lead more fulfilling lives

497. **Happy people live longer:** "Both positive affect (e.g., emotional well-being, positive mood, joy, happiness, vigor, energy) and positive trait-like dispositions (e.g., life satisfaction, hopefulness, optimism, sense of humor) were associated with reduced mortality in healthy population studies. Positive psychological well-being was significantly associated with reduced cardiovascular mortality in healthy population studies, and with reduced death rates in patients with renal failure and with human immunodeficiency virus-infection."

This was the result of a meta-analysis of 35 studies on initially healthy populations and 35 studies on populations suffering from endemic diseases. See "[Positive psychological well-being and mortality: a quantitative review of prospective observational studies](#)",[72] Y. Chida and A. Steptoe, *Psychosomatic Medicine*, September 2008.

498. **Happy people have more fulfilling lives:** Based on a meta-analysis of 225 papers, covering 275,000 people, results showed that "happy individuals are more likely than their less happy peers to have fulfilling marriages and relationships, high incomes, superior work performance, community involvement, robust health, and a long life". See "[The Benefits of Frequent Positive Affect: Does Happiness Lead to Success?](#)",[73] *Psychological Bulletin*, 2005, Sonja Lyubomirsky, Laura King and Ed Diener.

Individuals high in subjective well-being are more likely to secure job interviews, to be evaluated more positively by supervisors once they obtain a job, to show superior performance and productivity, and to handle managerial jobs better. They are also less likely to show counterproductive workplace behaviour and job burnout.

The benefits of gratitude

Do you take time to be grateful? There is clear evidence that this leads to greater happiness in a workplace, and long term success for the business.

499. **Gratitude leads to happiness:** A Hope College study[74] found that taking time to be grateful leads to greater hope and happiness for yourself. They explored the difference between gratefully remembering a past hope that had been fulfilled (in writing) and a control group who wrote no such report. Those who had written about being grateful found "significant increases in their hope and happiness".

500. **Gratitude leads to fewer GP visits:** In one study,[75] participants were divided into three groups and asked to write a few sentences a week about their feelings. One group wrote what they were grateful for, one group wrote what they were irritated by and one group simply wrote about anything that had affected them.

After 10 weeks, those who wrote about gratitude were overall more optimistic and felt better about their lives. Surprisingly, they also exercised more and had fewer visits to GPs than those who focused on sources of irritation. Report by Dr Robert A. Emmons of the University of California, Davis, and Dr Michael E. McCullough of the University of Miami.

501. **Thank people for their kindness:** One of the gurus of happiness psychology, Martin E. P. Seligman, found that[76] if you deliver a letter of gratitude to someone who has never been properly thanked for his or her kindness, the recipients immediately exhibited a huge increase in happiness scores.

Bibliography and Sources

Many of these ideas come from Happy clients and have been selected from examples they have given at our CEO breakfast, our Happy Workplaces webinars, or during courses or discussions with them. Other examples come from the speakers at our Happy Workplaces Conferences.

Further sources include a range of books. I love books that tell stories and give real examples, real nickables.

Bibliography

Many of these are truly inspirational. I particularly recommend *Maverick*, *Reinventing Organisations*, *Work Rules*, *Brave New Work*, *Multipliers* and *Make Work More Fun*. And, of course, *The Happy Manifesto*.

Becoming a Better Boss, Julian Birkinshaw
An employee's-eye view of what makes a great boss, and how you can become one, from LBS Professor Julian Birkinshaw, listed in the Thinkers50.

Work Rules, Laszlo Bock, 2015
"Insights from inside Google that will transform how you live and work," by Google's Head of People. A great insight into the culture of Google and packed with evidence-based approaches.

Winners, Alistair Campbell, 2015
Campbell (aide to Tony Blair) examines how winners tick and considers how they build great teams. A great insight into strategy.

It's the Manager, Jim Clifton, Jim Harper, 2019
Based on extensive surveys by Gallup, this gives detailed evidence on what works to create effective, productive organisations. The most important factor, as the title suggests, is the manager.

***Make Work More Fun*, Corporate Rebels**
Pioneering workplace practices from around the globe.

***The Joy of Work*, Bruce Daisley, 2019**
Ex-VP of Twitter, Bruce gives 30 practical examples that could help you become happier at work.

***The Age of Agile*, Stephen Denning, 2018**
How agile is moving beyond software and transforming organisations in the modern business world.

***CEO Excellence*, Carolyn Dewar, Scott Keller and Vikram Malhotra**
What do the best performing CEOs do?

***Brave New Work*, Aaron Dignan, 2019**
Are you ready to reinvent your organisation? A key work on self-managing organisations.

***Whoever Makes the Most Mistakes Wins*, Richard Farson with Ralph Keyes**
The paradox of innovation: the book argues that failure is a key factor in a path towards success.

***It Doesn't Have to be Crazy at Work*, Jason Fried and David Heinemeier Hansson, 2018**
The founders of software company Basecamp explain how they've created a company that avoids long hours and overwork, and instead encourages a life outside work.

***Superengaged*, Nikki Gatenby, 2018**
"How to transform business performance by putting people and purpose first".

***Mindful Work: How Meditation is Changing Business from the Inside Out*, David Gelles, 2015**
New York Times business reporter David Gelles explains how mindful managers are using meditation, yoga and other mindfulness techniques to boost leadership.

***Humanocracy*, Gary Hamel**

Gary Hamel is one of the lead figures in promoting self-managing organisations. In this book he describes how to replace bureaucracy with "humanocracy".

No Rules Rules, Reed Hastings and Erin Meyer, 2021
Reed and Erin describe the culture of Netflix, one of trust, freedom and critical feedback but also one where underperformance is met with a "generous severance package".

Delivering Happiness, Tony Hsieh, 2010
The CEO of Zappos explains how he built a radically different company, renowned for its fabulous customer service, based on focusing on the happiness of his people.

The Heart of Business, Hubert Joly
How Hubert turned around Best Buy and stopped trying to tell people what to do.

Leading with Happiness, Alexander Kjerulf, 2017
"How the best leaders put **happiness** first to create phenomenal business results and a better world", by Danish happiness guru Alexander Kjerulf.

Reinventing Organisations, Frederick Laloux, 2014
Again, a classic. Sub-title: *A Guide to Creating Organizations Inspired by the Next Stage of Human Consciousness*. This hugely influential book explores "Teal" organisations, those based on self-managing.

Team of Teams, General Stanley McChrystal, 2015
"The new rules of engagement for a complex world". McChrystal uses lessons from his own experience in Iraq and working for various companies to promote more empowered ways of working.

Employees First, Customers Second, Vineet Nayar, 2010
Vineet, CEO of HCL Technologies (an Indian outsourcing company employing over 70,000 people), explains his concept that if you focus on your employees, they in turn will focus on the customers.

A World Without Email, Cal Newport

Avoid the hive mind of continually responding to email (or to Slack or Teams) and do deep work.

Powerful, **Patty McCord, 2018**
McCord explains how, as Chief Talent Officer at Netflix, she helped create a high-performing culture based on freedom and responsibility.

*Mind Your F**king Business*, **Dom Monkhouse, 2023**
Get rid of performance appraisals, stop paying commission to your sales people and hire A-players.

Start-Up Factory, **Joost Minaar, Pim de Morree and Bran van der Lecq, 2022**
Haier's RenDanHeYi model and the end of management as we know it.

Becoming, **Michelle Obama, 2018**
Only mentioned here briefly but a powerful account from the ex-First Lady.

RADICAL Companies: Without Bosses or Employees, **Matt Perez and Adrian Perez, 2021**
The self-managing story of Nearsoft.

The Excellence Dividend, **Tom Peters, 2018**
"Meeting the tech tide with work that wows and jobs that last".

Happy as a Dane, **Malene Rydahl, 2017**
Ten secrets of the happiest people in the world.

How Google Works, **Eric Schmidt and Jonathan Rosenberg, 2014**
Ex-CEO Schmidt gives some great insights into the workings of the search giant.

Radical Candour, **Kim Scott, 2017**
As well promoting a kind of tough love, Kim gives great examples from her experience at Apple, Twitter and Google.

Maverick, **Ricardo Semler, 1993**

A classic. Brazilian businessman Ricardo Semler explains how he inherited his father's manufacturing business and turned it from a company with no trust to one where workers had the freedom to set their own targets, organise their workplaces, choose their managers and even – in some cases – set their own salaries.

The Happy Manifesto, Henry Stewart, 2013

The source of the ten principles included here. The book also contains many more stories and examples for each of these principles.

Things a Little Bird Told Me, Biz Stone, 2014

The story of Twitter from one of its co-founders.

Multipliers, Liz Wiseman, 2017

The acclaimed *Wall Street Journal* bestseller that explores why some leaders drain capability and intelligence from their teams while others amplify it to produce better results.

50 Transformational Practices, Worldblu, 2017

A playbook for building a world-class culture.

Blogs and podcasts

For the latest thinking we recommend:

My Happy blog: Check out my regular articles and posts on LinkedIn, and my blogs on the Happy website: https://bit.ly/HappyHenry

My podcast: This has more nickable ideas about how to create a happy workplace: www.happymanifesto.com

Corporate Rebels: Joost Minaar and Pim de Morree gave up their jobs to tour the world to find the most exciting workplaces on the planet, especially those featuring self-management. They write a must-read twice-weekly blog: https://corporate-rebels.com/

Lisa Gill, Reimaginaire: Lisa is at the forefront of self-managing organisations. Her blog is at https://medium.com/@reimaginaire and she has a monthly podcast at http://leadermorphosis.co/.

Alex Kjerulf: Writes a blog on happiness at work at https://positivesharing.com/

Dan Pink: The author of Drive, sign up to Dan's fortnightly newsletter, with a great one or two minute video: https://www.danpink.com/

Frederick Laloux: The author of *Reinventing Organisations* has a video series based on "pay-what-you-can": https://bit.ly/ReinventXX

Gary Hamel: A very insightful contributor, seeking to "light the fire of management innovation": http://www.garyhamel.com/blog

Index

3M, 115, 159
98%, 19
Aaron Dignan, 72, 118
AccessPlanIT, 129, 133
Adam Del Deo, 167
Adele Paterson, 129
Advanced Technology Services, 26
Advice Process, 32
Adviza, 25, 30, 35, 43, 51, 93, 95, 98, 99
AES, 55
Aetna, 132
AIESEC, 160
Alex Edmans, 182
Alex Kjerulf, 57, 110
Alexander Kjerulf, 41, 60, 109, 117, 124
Alison Kriel, 30
Alison Payne, 50
Alison Sturgess-Durden, 71, 147, 154, 173
Alistair Campbell, 70
Allen Carlson, 133
Allen Castro, 148
Amanda Gethin, 155
Anabal Montiel, 149
Andrew Barnes, 136
Andrew Chamberlain, 182
Anil Dash, 84
Annie Hagman, 127
Annie McDowall, 43
Apple, 72, 92, 151, 156, 158
Arlette Bentzen, 46, 47
Arsenal food store, 70
Arthur Fry, 159
ATS, 82, 148
Auzewell Chitewe, 44

B Corp, 118
B&Q, 30
Bank of America, 41
Barnaby Lashbrooke, 125
Basecamp, 67, 90, 96, 161, 162, 163, 164
Battle of Trafalgar, 17
Belgian Federal Office of Social Affairs, 85
Belgian Ministry of Social Security, 46, 64
Ben Hunt-Davis, 45
Ben Silbermann, 96
Bethlehem Steel, **45**
Bicycle, 124
Bill Gore, 141
Bill Hewlett, 18
Biz Stone, 45, 96, 118
Bloomberg, 111
Bon-Jin, 137
BP, 159
Brad Smith, 133
Breaks make sense, 130
broken arm, 128
Brooks Holton, **184**
Bruce Daisley, 123, 133
Buffer, 84
Buurtzorg, 37, 39, 56, 79, 153
Cal Newport, 24, 124
Carolyn Dewar, Scott Keller, and Vikram Malhotra, 111, 133, 150
Carrie Brandes, 50
Cary Cooper, 9
Cathy Busani, 44, 53, 88, 151, 164, 166
CC&R, 101

Celebrate MIstakes, 15
Center for leadership, 55
Chade Meng Tan, 131
Charles Schwab, 45
Charlie Kim, 101
Charlie Mayfield, 46
Chris MacQueen, 26
Chris May, 30, 101
Christian Krekel. *See* hristian Krekel
Clive Hutchinson, 158
CMI, 155
Coaches not managers, 153
Coca Cola, 109
Cocoon, 176
Colombia University, 181
Consent Decision Making, 33
Cook, 40, 41, 43, 47, 48, 50
Corporate Rebels, 36, 85
  Advice Process, 32
Cougar, 157
Cvent, **185**
Damien O'Neill, 27
Daniel Goleman, 179
Darren Childs, 77
David Gelles, 132
David Hoerman, 25
David Marquet, 29
David McCann, 182
DaVita, 25, 160
DBS, 133
Debbie Biondolillo, 156
Dennis Bakke, 55
Department of Health, 60
Derek Hill, 41, 42, 82, 99
Dick Costelo, 128
Dom Monkhouse, 23, 24, 26, 51, 54, 80, 88, 99, 111, 134, 145
Donna Reeves, 17, 30, 69, 147
Douglas MacGregor, 141
Dreamhost, 82
DreamHost, 156
East London Foundation Trust, 44
Elizabeth Medina, 181
Emily Dathan, 55
Engagement Institute, 179
Equal Experts, 32
Eric Schmidt, 88, 96, 116, 147, 156
Erin Meyer, 16, 23
Ernst & Young, 39
ESBZ, 57
Exeter, 128
EY, 130, 155
Facebook, 18, 93
FAVI, 156
Feedback
  Peer-to-peer, 55
Feike Sijbesma, 111
Fika, 127
First Community, 81
Frank Schmidt, 90
Frank van Massenhove, 85
Frederick Laloux, 33, 39, 51, 56, 57, 79, 129, 133, 156
Gallup, 53, 144, 164, 177, 179, 180, 182, 184
Gary Hamel, 26, 140, 173
GCHQ, 20, 66, 70
General Electric Appliances, 153
General Mills, 131
Geonetric, 66
George Marshall, 24, 124
Georgetown University, **184**
GitHub, 175

Glassdoor, 182
Glebe retirement community, 137
Glitch, 84
Golden Rule, 43
Google, 50, 69, 87, 93, 97, 110, 113, 115, 123, 131, 147, 151, 152, 159, 177
Guy Hayward, 139
Hackney Council, 55
Haier, 36, 58, 79, 120, 153
Hal Rosenbluth, 59
Happy, 13, 24, 32, 35, 44, 53, 55, 66, 71, 78, 84, 94, 97, 98, 99, 100, 126, 128, 129, 138, 151, 155, 157, 164, 165, 176
Happy Workplace Leadership Programme, 145
Harry Truman, 124
Harvard Business Review, **185**
Harvard Business School, 127
Havering Sixth Form College, 34
Hay Group, 157, **184**
HCL, 59, 71, 72, 78, 79
HealthWatch Central West London, 132
Heart of Kent Hospice, 149
Heiligenfeld, 129
Helen Sanderson, 43, 54
Henley Business School, 136
Henry James, 43
Henry Searl, 42
Herb Kelleher, 34, 59
Hewlett-Packard, 16, 18
HIPPO, 29

Hope College, **187**
Hubert Joly, 31, 42, 148, 165
Huntsman, 108
Hyatt Hotel, 69
IIH Denmark, 136
Innocent, 153
Intel, 131
Intuit, 108
James Dyson, 110
James Quincey, 109
Jan Carlzon, 18, 77
Jason Fried and David Heinemeier Hansson, 68, 90, 97, 133
Jeff Bezos, 125
Jennifer Nierva, 16
Jim Clifton, Jim Harper, 40, 53, 54, 71, 157, 164
Jim Clifton, Jim Harter, 144, 152
John Housego, 77, 100, 141
John Hunter, 90
John Lewis Partnership, 41, 46, 50, 123
John Maynard Keynes, 135
John Quincy Adams, 160
John Timpson, 16, 21, 64, 87, 117, 148, 152
JOMO, 163
Jon Clifton, 179
Jony Ive, 72
Jos de Blok, 38, 153
Joy, 54
Julian Birkinshaw, 31
Julie Zhou, 93
Kamal Birdi, 177
Kate Collins, 54
Katharine Horler, 35
Katherine Billingham-Mohammed, 52

Katherine Horler, 25, 30, 41, 43, 51, 93, 95, 98, 99
Kevin Rogers, 30
Kevin Systrom, 96
Kim Scott, 72, 96, 113, 128, 148, 159, 165
Kings Fund, 183
Kirsten Regal, 133
Larry Page, 110
Laszlo Bock, 23, 50, 52, 67, 69, 80, 88, 90, 93, 97, 110, 115, 152, 177
Laurence Vanhee, 46, 64, 101
Lawrence Parkin, 52
Learning Nexus, 52
Lindsey Van Driel, 131
Liz Mouland, 81
Liz Wiseman, 29, 144, 149
Long Hours, 125
Louise Beardmore, 28, 69, 82
Luke Kyte, 51, 73, 94
Lydia Theaker, 14
Macquarie Telecom, 108
Malene Rydahl, 69
Marc Zuckerberg, 18
Marco Nink, 180
Marcus Buckingham, 165
Marshall Goldsmith, 148
Martin Banck, 139
Martin E. P. Seligman, 187
Maryella Gockel, 130
Mastercard, 159
Matt Smalley, 129, 133
Mayden, 30, 101, 154, 173, 174
McKinsey, 101
McKinsey & Company, 22
Me Time, 126
Medium, 175
Menlo Innovations, 96, 110
Mervyn Kaye, 129
Michael Bloomberg, 111
Michael Davies, 108
Michelle Hill, 20
Michelle Obama, 67
Microsoft, 130
Microsoft Japan, 135
Mike Markulla, 158
Mindvalley, 49, 81
Morning Star, 54, 78, 173
National Audit Office, 21
Nearsoft, 65, 149
Nelson, 17
Netflix, 16, 17, 23, 110, 149, 167, 168, 169, 170, 171
New Belgium Brewing, 80
Next Jump, 57, 102
NextJump, 42, 52, 87, 111, 117, 126
Nicole Martin, 126
Nigel Baptiste, 23
Nikki Gatenby, 45, 48, 49, 50, 59, 99, 123
Nixon McInnes, 35, 111
Noelle Nelson, **185**
Nordstrom, 69
North West Care Cooperative, 175
Northwold Primary School, 30
Nucor, 79
OKRs, 114
Olivia Clymer, 132
OneShot, 20
Orpheus Chamber Orchestra, 160
Ozvision, 50
Patty McCord, 17, 68, 148

Paul Wakeling, 34
Paycare, 30
Perpetual Guardian, 136
Peter Drucker, 19, 129
Pixar, 82, 83
Platinum Rule, 43
Pluristem, 150
Polly Neate, 51
Praxis, 133
President Eisenhower, 24
Pret a Manger, 92
Project Oxygen, 152
Propellernet, 45, 48, 49, 50, 59, 99
Psychological Bulletin, **186**
Psychosomatic Medicine, **186**
Queens School of Business, 180
Quiet Space, 126
Rachel Simmons, 111
Rachel Street, 124, 149
Rackspace, 23, 26, 88, 99, 111
Rajan Tata, 110
Rebecca Dobson, 145
Recruit for Attitude, 15
Reddico, 51, 73, 76, 94
Reed Hastings, 16, 23, 65, 110, 149
Ricardo Semler, 13, 61
Richard Sheridan, 92, 96, 110
Ritz Carlton, 21
Robert Altman, 150
Robert Emmons, 187
Robert Sutton, Ben Wigert, 53
Robert Tomasko, 159
Roche, 31
Rolls-Royce, 159
Rosie Brown, 40, 43, 47
Royal DSM, 111
Russell Findlay, 57
Salar Kamangar, 96
Salesforce, 31
Sally Daglian, 133
Sandy Pentland, 41
Sarah Gillard, 41, 50, 123
Sarah Pugh, 52, 89
SAS, 18
SAS Airline, 77
Saskia Gheysens, 86
Scott Cook, 108
Scott Darrugh, 21
SEB, 47
Semco, 61, 93
Share Community, 43
Shawn Achor, **185**
Shelter, 51
Sheryl Sandberg, 167
Simon Biltcliffe, 52
Smiling is contagious, 41
Smith College, 110
Snapshot, 53
Sonia Lyubomirsky, **185**
Sonja Lyubomirsky, **186**
Sophie Bryan, 54
Southbank Centre, 94
Southwest Airlines, 34, 59
Speakers Trust, 57
Spedan Lewis, 46
Stanford University, 125
Stanley McChrystal, 17, 21, 41, 69, 79, 134
Stay interview, 102
Stephen Denning, 78, 79, 96
Stephen Kosslyn, 165
Steve Hedley, 51
Steve Jobs, 72, 83, 92, 158

Steve Wozniak, 158
Stoke Newington School, 90
Stop, Start, Continue, 55
Strengthfinder, 164
Stroke Associatio, 25
Sun, 133
Sun Hydraulics, 133
Takuya Hirano, 135
Tarun Gidoomal, 42, 87, 102, 111
Tata, 110
Ted Sarandos, 167
Teenage Cancer Trust, 54
Thank you, 41
Timpsons, 16, 21, 64, 87, 117, 148, 152
TLC, 20
TNT, 51
Tom Peters, 59, 70, 108, 124, 129, 150, 151
Tony Hsieh, 18, 93
Toyota, 103, 105, 107, 139
Transparency, 78
Trinity, 51
Trust people, 14
Twitter, 45, 128
u2i, 174
Ubiquity, 50
UKTV, 77, 81
Ulysses Lyons, 17
United Utilities, 27, 69, 81

University of Alberta, **184**
University of California, 187
University of Sheffield, 177
US schools, 137
Vala Afshar, 31
Valve, 175
Vineet Nayar, 59, 78, 79
Virgin Atlantic, 97
Vishan Lacklani, 81
W. Edwards Deming, 67, 106
Warwick University, **184**
Webmart, 52
WebMart, 49
Wellbeing Teams, 43
Wharton Business School, 182
white envelope, 101
Whitehall Study, 183
Whizz Kidz, 88
Wills Tower Watson, 179
WL Gore, 18, 77, 100, 109, 140, 142, 155
WooHoo, 46, 47
Woowa Brothers, 137
Worldblu, 35, 65, 71, 80, 81, 82, 156, 160
Yaky Yaney, 150
Yoichi Chida, **186**
Yvonne Agnei, 87, 88
Zappos, 17, 57, 93, 174

The Happy MBA

Many MBAs are based on finance and strategy. Ours is based on people. If you would like a two-year programme of transformational discovery, this could be for you.

Our Level 7 Senior Leaders programme will help you create a workplace culture based on trust and freedom using all the ideas in this book.

If you are based in England, then the full cost of the programme can be taken from the Apprenticeship Levy. If your organisation doesn't pay the levy then it is 95% funded by the government, so the cost is just £700. Check it out at https://bit.ly/HappyLevel7.

We also have Level 3 programmes for Team Leaders and Level 5 programmes for Operational Managers.

(Note, though we like to call it the Happy MBA, it is not accredited by a university, though Level 7, the Senior Leaders programme, is the equivalent of an MA.)

How to Contact Happy

Happy Ltd does many things. We train people to use IT, making learning about computers a fun and involving process. And, in our Happy People division, we help organisations create great workplaces.

Happy People is the fastest growing part of the business. We find there is a real hunger and a real eagerness to learn how you make somewhere a great place to work. Most companies now realise that being a great workplace will make them more effective and give them a competitive advantage in the marketplace.

We can help your organisation. If it is already doing well, we believe we can make it even more effective. And, if it's a lousy place to work in, we'd love to help you transform it. Contact us now:

Happy People
9 Alie Street
London
E1 8DE
020 7375 7300
happypeople@happy.co.uk

www.happy.co.uk

Or contact me directly. I'm at henry@happy.co.uk and my mobile phone number is 07870 682442. I'd love to hear what you think of the ideas in this book. Just please don't use these contact details to try and sell me anything!

Are you a CEO who believes in happy workplaces?

If so, at Happy we have a free CEO breakfast each month. Find out more by emailing me at henry@happy.co.uk

We also have an HR breakfast. Again email me for details.

Notes

[1] Facebook 10,000 versions: https://bit.ly/EntZuck
[2] DaVita leaders: https://bit.ly/IncDaVita
[3] David Marquet: https://bit.ly/MarquetSub
[4] Corporate Rebels Advice Process: https://bit.ly/CRAdvice
[5] South West Airlines: https://bit.ly/SWfriendly
[6] Smile Research: https://bit.ly/BCSmile
[7] MindValley Love Week: https://bit.ly/LoveWeekx
[8] Next Jump dance battle: http://bit.ly/3nHKfCk
[9] Performance Reviews suck: https://bit.ly/PRSucks
[10] Solicited advice is better than unsolicited: https://bit.ly/4O08v08
[11] Ricardo Semler: Managing without managers: https://bit.ly/SemlerManage
[12] GCHQ: Innovate Day: https://bit.ly/InnovateDay
[13] Pixar: Freedom: https://bit.ly/PIXfreedom
[14] Buffer salaries: https://bit.ly/3Ki7NVY
[15] Glitch salaries: https://bit.ly/3Ki7NVY
[16] Semco democratic vote: http://bit.ly/43eam40
[17] Virgin swimming policy: https://bit.ly/VirginSw
[18] Onsite Insights programme: https://onsiteinsights.org/
[19] Netflix cancel shows: https://bit.ly/NetCancel
[20] *New York Times*, Smith College: https://bit.ly/NYfailure
[21] Corporate Rebels, Haier: http://bit.ly/3KFGE0T
[22] Chinese Companies, Management, HBR, https://bit.ly/3UFj73n
[23] Stanford long hours research: https://bit.ly/StandfordLong
[24] Harvard Business School reflection study: https://bit.ly/15Reflect
[25] Microsoft, taking breaks makes sense: http://bit.ly/41o5qYz
[26] Microsoft Japan 4-day week: https://bit.ly/MS4days
[27] Perpetual 4-day week: https://bit.ly/Perpetual4
[28] Andrew Barnes 4-day week video (13 mins): https://bit.ly/Barnes4x
[29] IIH 4-day week video (3 mins): https://bit.ly/IIH4Day
[30] Henley Business School, 4-day research: https://bit.ly/Henley4
[31] UK opinion poll, 4-day week: https://bit.ly/Wired4
[32] Sweden, Toyota, 6-hour day: https://bit.ly/SwedenToyota
[33] W. L. Gore, *FT*, 2008: https://bit.ly/WLGoreBosses
[34] W. L. Gore, *Financial Times*, 2019

[35] W. L. Gore, *Wall Street Journal*, Gary Hamel: https://bit.ly/WLGoreHamel
[36] John Housego, 2015 Happy Workplaces Conference: https://bit.ly/JohnHousego
[37] Gallup, State of the American Manager: https://bit.ly/GallupState
[38] Managers cause stress: http://bit.ly/43pI7zC

[40] Inc, Basecamp, no managers: https://bit.ly/IncNoManagers
[41] Gallup, playing to strengths: https://bit.ly/GallupState
[42] LinkedIn post, Not Busy: https://bit.ly/NotBusyNetflix
[43] HBR, Morning Star, Gary Hamel: https://bit.ly/HamelFire
[44] Mayden, flat structure: https://bit.ly/MaydenFlat
[45] U2i, Corporate Rebels: https://www.corporate-rebels.com/blog/u2i
[46] Valve Employee Handbook: https://bit.ly/3mjltZ1
[47] Valve Anarco-syndicalism https://bit.ly/IncNoManagers
[48] Scaling GitHub: https://bit.ly/ScalingGitHub
[49] Medium, No Managers: https://bit.ly/MediumNo
[50] Cocoon, https://bit.ly/CocoonNo
[51] CMI poll about managers: https://bit.ly/CMIManagers
[52] Willis Tower Watson, Power of 3: https://bit.ly/Power3x
[53] Cost of £450 to $550 billion a year: https://bit.ly/NoLaughx
[54] Germany, Gallup, sickness: https://bit.ly/LowSickness
[55] Gallup, State of the American Workplace 2017: https://bit.ly/Gall2017
[56] Job Satisfaction, Colombia University: https://bit.ly/JobCul
[57] Alex Edmans, does the job market fully value intangibles: https://bit.ly/EdmansX
[58] Treat employees well, stock markets will soar: https://bit.ly/TreatXX
[59] Glassdoor best place to work list: https://bit.ly/Glassdoor20
[60] Gallup, State of the American Workplace 2017: https://bit.ly/Gall2017
[61] Fewer patients die in happy hospitals: http://bit.ly/3nV6xAC
[62] More control over your work makes you healthier: https://bit.ly/WhitehallX
[63] Greater customer loyalty and higher productivity:

https://bit.ly/Economist19
[64] Happy workers are less likely to leave: https://bit.ly/3zLWGjt
[65] University of Alberta, focus on meaning: http://bit.ly/41gkPu4
[66] Hay Group, engage your employees for a competitive advantage: http://bit.ly/3KpV3gd
[67] Be happy and be more productive: http://bit.ly/3mxuw8C
[68] Shawn Achor, Positive Intelligence: https://bit.ly/3oiUpK4
[69] Lyubomirsky: Benefits of frequent positive affect: https://bit.ly/3ZYKM0f
[70] Focus on employee wellbeing: http://bit.ly/43qgHtu
[71] Customer retention rates higher when employees engaged: http://bit.ly/40WIT5n
[72] Happy people live longer: http://bit.ly/3mpiZbz
[73] Happy people have more fulfilling lives: https://bit.ly/3ZYKM0f
[74] Gratitude leads to happiness: https://buff.ly/2xpKxUB
[75] Gratitude leads to fewer GP visits: https://bit.ly/3Kr538U
[76] Thank people for their kindness: http://bit.ly/3Kr538U

Printed in Great Britain
by Amazon